Richard Sorger & Jenny Udale

THE
FUNDAMENTALS
OF FASHION
DESIGN

ava | Academia
the environment of learning

An AVA Book
Published by AVA Publishing SA
Rue des Fontenailles 16
Case Postale
1000 Lausanne 6
Switzerland

Tel: +41 786 005 109
Email: enquiries@avabooks.ch

Distributed by Thames & Hudson (ex-North America)
181a High Holborn
London WC1V 7QX
United Kingdom

Tel: +44 20 7845 5000
Fax: +44 20 7845 5055
Email: sales@thameshudson.co.uk
www.thamesandhudson.com

Distributed in the USA & Canada by:
Watson-Guptill Publications
770 Broadway
New York, New York 10003
USA

Fax: 1-646-654-5487
Email: info@watsonguptill.com
www.watsonguptill.com

English Language Support Office
AVA Publishing (UK) Ltd.

Tel: +44 1903 204 455
Email: enquiries@avabooks.co.uk

ISBN 2-940373-39-6 and 978-2-940373-39-0

10 9 8 7 6 5 4 3 2

Design by Sifer Design

www.siferdesign.co.uk

Cover photography by Sifer Design

Index by Indexing Specialists (UK) Ltd.

Production by AVA Book Production Pte. Ltd., Singapore

Tel: +65 6334 8173
Fax: +65 6259 9830
Email: production@avabooks.com.sg

Richard Sorger & Jenny Udale

THE
FUNDAMENTALS
OF FASHION
DESIGN

Contents

3

CONSTRUCTION

4

DEVELOPING A COLLECTION

5

THE FASHION MACHINE

Interviews with...

How to get the most out of this book

The Fundamentals of Fashion Design is intended to be a solid foundation for those who work, develop and study within fashion. Through guidance, photography and illustration, key areas of fashion development are covered, such as, how to generate ideas, develop and promote collections. This book offers a unique resource and insight into the practical, philosophical and professional world of fashion design.

1

Section colour key

Denotes the chapter and also signifies the start of a new section.

2

Group captions

Related imagery is pulled together in factual form.

3

Box-outs

Illustrate key information.

4

Images

Images from a vast range of international designers bring the text to life.

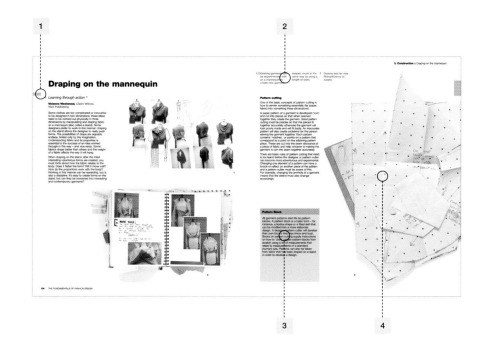

1   **Additional Illustrations**

Contain a wealth of interesting facts and diagrammatic information.

2   **Body copy**

In-depth discussion of working methods and best practice, including professional advice guidance.

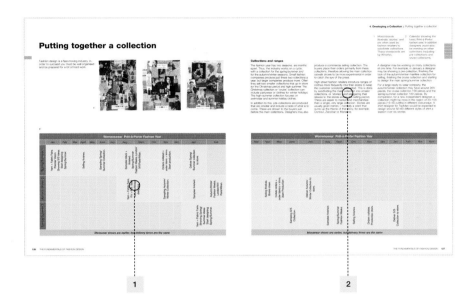

1

2

1   **Interviews**

Feature expert, in-depth knowledge and advice from some of today's finest fashion designers.

2   **Pull-quotes**

Highlight key points from professional designers.

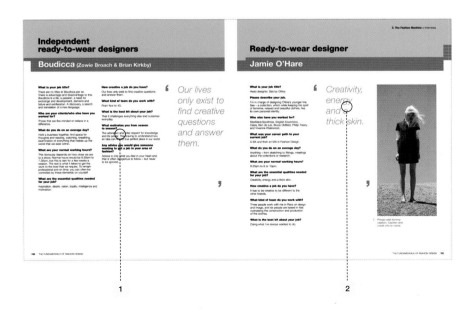

1

2

Introduction

Fashion is merely a form of ugliness so unbearable that we are compelled to alter it every six months.

Oscar Wilde

Oscar Wilde was passionate about his appearance and his clothes, so it is perhaps with his tongue planted firmly in his cheek that he made the above remark. We are drawn to fashion, not only as a means to express ourselves individually by the way we dress, but also as a method of creative expression through design.

Fashion is a constant search for the new. It is hungry and ruthless. But to be able to create clothes is also very exciting and very rewarding.

In this book we will introduce you to the fundamental principles of fashion design. Designers do not just sit at a desk and design pretty frocks. They need to research and develop a theme, source fabrics and develop a cohesive range with them. A good designer understands the differing properties of fabric and what is achievable with them, and an understanding of the techniques of garment construction is essential to fashion design. When developing a collection, a designer needs to think about whom they are designing for, what type of garments they are developing and for what season.

The finished collection of garments is only the start; it then has to be promoted and marketed. A fashion designer is only one of many jobs in the fashion industry. Not everyone with a love of fashion has the ability to be a talented designer. It might be that you find you are more suited to another career within the fashion industry. There are creative people with a love of fashion who are fashion buyers, selling agents, journalists, photographers, stylists, illustrators, and all of these people are essential to the success of the fashion designer.

The Fundamentals of Fashion Design is packed with varied examples of work by talented designers and others in the fashion industry, used to illustrate the no-nonsense text and to inspire you.

We hope that you enjoy it...

RESEARCH AND DESIGN

" Fashion Design, according to Vivienne Westwood is "almost like mathematics".
You have a vocabulary of ideas which you have to add and subtract in order
to come up with an equation right for the times. "

Vivienne Westwood: An Unfashionable Life, Jane Mulvagh

1

Are you fashionable?

There is no point trying to be fashionable. This book cannot tell you how to design fashion; it can only tell you what the ingredients are, ways to put them together, and many of the important things you must consider when designing clothes. Clothing is only 'fashionable' when your peers or the industry deem a design to be of the zeitgeist. It either is or it isn't.

The Oxford English Dictionary defines fashion as 'current popular custom or style, especially in dress'. Essentially it means a style that is up to date, and how this is agreed upon is subjective and reliant on a number of factors. For instance, the punk movement was a reflection of how many young people were feeling in the late 1970s – disenchanted with the politics and culture of the time – and was somewhat engineered by Malcolm McLaren and designer Vivienne Westwood. Not that the punk movement set out to be 'fashionable' – anything but! Its aim was to be peripheral, subversive. But this reinforces the idea that trying too hard should not be a factor.

Exhibitions, films and music can have a huge influence on what is deemed fashionable at a given time. In 2001, Baz Luhrmann's movie, *Moulin Rouge*, had a direct influence on the catwalk and many designers looked to burlesque for inspiration that season. Dior Homme's designer Hedi Slimane has cited controversial Babyshambles singer Pete Doherty as an influence, even publishing a book of photographs of the singer.

For fashion design, it is important to develop an awareness of your own taste and style (not how you dress – designers are often the worst dressed in a room because they are too busy thinking about how to dress others). Not everyone has an aptitude or desire to design 'unconventional' clothes. Some designers focus on the understatement or detail of garments. Other designers design 'conventional' garments, but it is the way they are put together (or styled) that makes the outfit original and modern. Knowing what you are best at is essential, but doesn't mean that you should not experiment. It can take a while to 'know yourself' and this period of discovery is usually spent at college. There has to be a certain amount of soul searching; it's not so much being the designer that you want to be, but rather finding out the designer that you are. You must be true to your own vision of how you want to dress someone.

Beyond that, the rest is in the hands of the industry and the fashion-buying public to decide, and for every person who likes your work there will be someone who really doesn't. This is common and working in such a subjective field can be confusing, but eventually you will learn to navigate your way through criticism and either develop a steely exterior or recognise which opinions you respect and which to disregard. Once you accept this, you are free to get on with what you are best at – designing clothes.

1 Vivienne Westwood wearing her 'Destroy' T-shirt.

1

Know your subject

If a career in fashion is what you want then you need to know your subject. This might appear to be an obvious statement, but it must be said. You may protest, 'but I don't want to be influenced by other designers' work'. Of course not, but unless you know what has preceded you, how do you know that you aren't naively reproducing someone else's work?

Making yourself 'fashion aware' doesn't happen overnight, and, if you're passionate about the subject it is natural to want to find out about it (that's why you've picked up this book). If you are applying to a university or college to study fashion, your interview panel will want you to demonstrate that you have a rudimentary knowledge of designers and their styles. You may even be asked who you like and dislike in order to qualify your answer.

Magazines are a good place to start, but don't just automatically reach for *Elle* and *Vogue*. There are many more magazines out there, each appealing to a different niche market and style subculture and you should have a knowledge of as many as possible; they are all part of the fashion machine.

Magazines will not only make you aware of different designers, but so-called lifestyle magazines will also make you aware of other design industries and cultural events that often influence (or will be influenced by) fashion. By regularly reading magazines you will also become aware of stylists, journalists, fashion photographers and hair and make-up artists, models, muses, brands and shops that are all-important to the success of a fashion designer.

There are also some great websites that show images of outfits on the catwalk almost as soon as the show has taken place. One such site, www.style.com, is free.

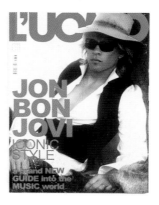

1

1   There are numerous
fashion and lifestyle
magazines that will
inform and inspire
your own work.

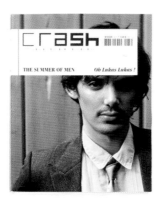

Starting your research

Designers are like magpies, always on the look out for something to use or steal! Fashion moves incredibly fast compared to other creative industries and it can feel like there is constant pressure to reinvent the wheel each season. Designers need to be continually seeking new inspiration in order to keep their work fresh, contemporary, and above all, to keep themselves stimulated.

In this sense, research means creative investigation, and good design can't happen without some form of research. It feeds the imagination and inspires the creative mind.

Research takes two forms. The first kind is sourcing material and practical elements. Many fledgling designers forget that finding fabrics and other ingredients – rivets, fastenings or fabric treatments, for example – must make up part of the process of research and having an appreciation of what is available, where from, and for how much, is essential.

The second form of research is the kind you make once you've found a theme or concept for use in your designs. Themes can be personal, abstract or more literal. Alexander McQueen, Vivienne Westwood and John Galliano have designed collections where the sources of inspiration are clear for anyone to see. McQueen's 'It's A Jungle Out There' 1997–1998 collection mixed religious painting with the evocation of an endangered African antelope. Westwood has drawn on pirates, the paintings of Fragonard and 17th- and 18th-century decorative arts in the Wallace Collection for inspiration in different collections. Galliano has been influenced by the circus, ancient Egypt, punk singer Siouxsie Sioux and the French Revolution.

Designers may also convey a mood or use a muse for inspiration. Galliano currently cites singer Gwen Stefani as a muse, but has also based collections around 1920s' dancer Josephine Baker and Napoleon's Empress Josephine.

Using a theme or concept makes sense because it will hold together the body of work, giving it continuity and coherence. It also sets certain boundaries – which of course the designer is free to break – but having a theme initially gives the designer focus.

With a collection, how do you decide on a theme?

Throughout there is discussion, arguments, discovery and curiosity.

What is your approach to research?

It is an ongoing dialogue that you have with yourself and those around you, a constant search for knowledge. Within that search you come across questions that need more development and that you may have no answer for. It is then that you go on this quest for visual and intellectual answers that somehow create a new question, a language that may answer or leave you with confusion.

What do you want to express through clothes?

A journey, a feeling of tomorrow.

What is your approach to the design process?

This is the further ascension into three-dimensional dialogue between idea and executioner. The base of a two-dimensional idea is honest, but also only begins the process. Then the design journey begins by weaving a web of ideas, silhouettes, fabric, colours, textures, and sound even can develop your thoughts towards design. There is a final vision and the design process works outwards through all the media mentioned.

1   Christian Dior haute couture Spring/Summer collection 2004.

1

Choosing a concept

When choosing a theme, be honest. It needs to be something that you can work and live with for the duration of the collection. This means that it should be a subject that you are interested in, that stimulates you and that you understand. Some designers prefer to work with an abstract concept that they want to express through the clothing (for example, 'isolation'), while others want to use something more visually orientated (such as 'the circus').

Either of these approaches is appropriate and it is about choosing which works for you. But it does need to work for you; it is pointless choosing a theme that doesn't inspire you. If the ideas are still struggling to come after a certain point a clever designer will be honest and question their choice of theme.

Remember, press and buyers are generally only interested in the outcome. Do the clothes look good? Do they flatter? Do they excite? Will they sell? They are not necessarily interested how well you've managed to express quantum physics through a jacket. But if this is what you want to express, then do it.

1   Choose your theme
    or concept carefully
    as it should be a help
    to designing, not a
    hindrance.

1

Sources of research

Where to go to begin your research depends on your theme or concept. For an enquiring designer the act of researching is like detective work, hunting down elusive information and subject material that will ignite a spark.

The easiest place to start to research is on the Internet. The Web is a fantastic source of images and information. It is also great for sourcing fabrics direct from manufacturers that produce specialist material or companies that perform specific services.

A good library is a treasure. Local libraries are geared to provide books to a broad cross-section of the community so tend to have a few books about many subjects. Specialist libraries are the most rewarding, and the older the library the better – books that are long out of print will (hopefully) still be on the shelves, or at least viewable upon request. Colleges and universities should have a library geared towards the courses that are being taught, though access may be restricted if you are not actually studying there.

Flea markets and antique fairs are useful sources of inspirational objects and materials for designers. It goes without saying that clothing of any kind, be it antique or contemporary, can inspire more clothes. Historic, ethnic or specialist clothing – military garments, for example – offer insight into details, methods of manufacture and construction that you may not have encountered before.

1

2   3

1   A Marc Jacobs's jacket inspired by military clothing (2/3).

4   Vivienne Westwood pirate shirt and sash.

5   Illustration of pirates. Vivienne Westwood researched the cut of pirate clothing for her pirate collection Autumn/Winter 1981/82.

Like flea markets, charity shops are great places to find clothes, books, records and bric-a-brac that, in the right hands and with a little imagination, could prove inspirational. Everyday objects that are no longer popular or are perceived as kitsch can be appropriated, rediscovered and used ironically to design clothes.

Museums, such as London's Victoria and Albert Museum, not only collect and showcase interesting objects from around the world, both historical and contemporary, but also have an excellent collection of costume that can be viewed upon request.

Large companies, with the budget, send their designers on research trips, often abroad, to search for inspiration. There, the designers are armed with a research budget and a camera, and can record and buy anything that might prove useful for the coming season. Designers with a tight budget might use a holiday abroad as a similar opportunity.

Sources of images can be photocopies, postcards, photographs, tearsheets from magazines and drawings. But anything can be used for research: images, fabrics, details such as buttons or an antique collar – anything that inspires you qualifies as research. Whichever items you collect must be within easy reach (and view) so that you have your reference constantly about you.

4

5

The research book

As a designer you will eventually develop an individual approach to 'processing' this research. Some designers collect piles of photocopies and fabrics that may find their way on to a wall in the studio. Others compile research or sketch-books where images, fabrics and trimmings are collected and collated, recording the origin and evolution of a collection. Still others take the essence of the research and produce what are called mood-, theme- or storyboards.

A research book is not necessarily solely for the designer's use. Showing research to other people is useful when trying to convey the themes of a collection. It might be used to communicate your concept to your tutor, your employers, employees or a stylist.

Research books are not just scrapbooks. A scrapbook infers that the information is collected, but unprocessed. There is nothing duller than looking through pages of lifeless, rectangular images that have been (too) carefully cut out. It is also debatable how much the designer has gleaned from creating pages like this. A research book should reflect the thought processes and personal approach to the project. It becomes more personal when it is drawn on and written in, and when the images and materials that have been collected are manipulated or collaged.

1

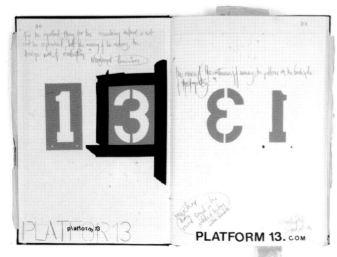

2

3

1/2 Boudicca's research
3/4 books are developed
around an ongoing
dialogue between the
designers and with
others in a constant
search for knowledge.

Their research is
very much about
pursuing a trail of
questions and
answers that is
both visual and
intellectual.

5/6 Other examples of
research books.

Collage

The word 'collage' is derived from the French
word for glue. A good collage is where the
separate elements (images) work on different
levels at the same time, to form both a whole
and also its individual component parts.
Successful collages usually include a bricolage
of different-sized, differently sourced images that
provide a stimulating visual rhythm.

4

5

6

Mood-, theme- and storyboards

Mood-, theme- and storyboards are essentially a distillation of research. In a sense they are the 'presentation' version of the research book. They are made up as collages, and, as the name suggests, generally mounted on board, which makes them more durable. They are used by a designer to communicate the themes, concepts, colours and fabrics that will be used to design the season's collection. They may include key words that convey a 'feeling', such as 'comfort' or 'seduction'. If the collection must be tailored to a particular client, the images may be more specifically attuned to the perceived lifestyle/identity of the potential client.

1 The fabrication and colour on this mood-board are inspired by the images behind; the acquatic image evokes transparent and fluid fabrics. The feathered corsage suggests fractured colours and a dot design.

I never saw any point in stopping at the way in which a conventional wisdom decreed a jacket should be cut. Early on, I realised how important it is just to be curious. You mustn't be frightened or hide behind pre-conceived ideas. You have to experiment. You just do it and it's beautiful because you discover an energy there which feeds you. There are no rules.

John Galliano, from *Galliano* by Colin McDowell, **Weidenfeld & Nicolson**

1

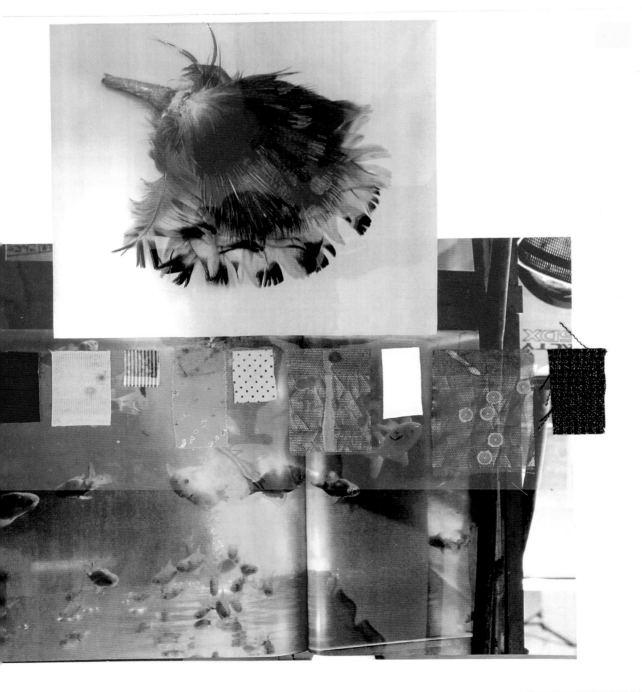

Ideal bodies

Historically, fashionable clothing was designed to enhance and idealise the natural silhouette of the human form by exaggerating parts of the body. The 'ideal' body shape continues to be based on an 'hourglass'. However, today, most clothes follow the line of the body itself and the fashionable silhouette is less enhanced than it was before. Perhaps this is because it is easier than ever to forego aids such as the corset or bustle and to alter the body itself by living a healthy lifestyle or making use of cosmetic surgery. But the evolution of the silhouette also relates to changing social and cultural trends.

1

1 These examples show off typical Victorian hourglass figures.

2 Examples of corsets and hooped skirts with bustles that when worn exaggerate the buttocks.

Nip and tuck

The corset, as we know it, has been worn by women – and men – since the early part of the 16th century. Since that time various contraptions have been added to corsets to exaggerate the hips and buttocks in different ways. Petticoats, farthingales, panniers, crinolines and bustles are all contraptions that have been fashionable at different times in the last five hundred years to accentuate the shapeliness of the human body and to project a shifting ideal of the female and male form.

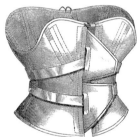

2

Dior's 'New Look' collection of 1947 was a response to the stringent use of fabrics during the war years and a conscious feminisation of the female form. It was defined by the generous use of luxurious fabrics and an accentuated wasp-waisted silhouette with widely flared skirts over padded hips, and its influence endured all through the 1950s.

Corsets have also affected the shape of the chest, from the cleavage of the 18th and 19th centuries through to the mono bosom of the early 20th century. The supported chest reached a climax with the torpedo-like girdles and bras of the late 1940s and 1950s, revived and refigured in Jean-Paul Gaultier's signature bra tops of the early 1990s.

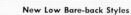

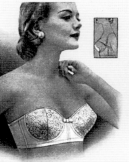

1

2

1/2 Typical clothing of
  the 1950s, as pictured
  in Sears catalogues.

3 Illustrations by
  the French fashion
  illustrator Erté
  portraying the typical
  1920s' silhouette.

In the 1920s and later in the 1960s, fashionable women adopted a radical silhouette that subverted the hourglass form. The 1920s' silhouette was less constrained than what had preceded it – although, perversely, curvier women were required to artificially flatten their bodies with tube-like bandeaux in order to fit with the times. The 1960s' silhouette went hand-in-hand with the trend for a more boyish look. Fashionable women wore their hair short, and, if they were lucky, they already had flat chests, narrow shoulders and hips which complemented miniskirts and dresses.

Another example of an enhanced silhouette that was hugely popular in the 1980s and 1990s was the use of exaggerated shoulder pads in what became coined at the time as 'power dressing'. The exaggerated shape became synonymous with strength, authority and the excesses of capitalism. The large pads allowed unstructured garments to hang from them, but as garments became more fitted the triangulation became more extreme. Giorgio Armani was a designer heavily associated with this look.

3

Silhouette

Our first impression of an outfit when it emerges on the catwalk is formed by its silhouette, which means that we look at its overall shape before we interrogate the detail, fabric or texture of the garment.

Silhouette is a fundamental consideration in your decision making. Which parts of the body do you want to emphasise and why? A full skirt will draw attention to the waist, forming an arrow shape between waist and hem. Wide shoulders produce the same result and can also make the hips look narrower. The waist itself does not have to be fixed as it is anatomically placed. It can be displaced through curved side seams or the raising or lowering of a horizontal (waist) line. The silhouette can also be affected by using fabric to create volume around the body or by making it close-fitting to accentuate it.

Choosing the size of a shoulder pad or where the waist is accentuated may seem like small decisions to make, but these subtle choices about silhouette give your clothes a unifying identity and stop them from becoming generic shapes. For example, Alexander McQueen's early collections in the 1990s suggested strong female sexuality and power through severe, close-fitted tailoring and shoulder pads that formed right angles to the neck. At a time when other designers were avoiding excessive shoulder pads because of their connotations with the 1980s and early 1990s, McQueen's shoulder line was aggressive and bold.

1   Australian performance artist, fashion designer and icon, Leigh Bowery. (Photograph Courtesy of Fergus Greer and Perry Rubenstein Gallery)

1

'No' Pantsuit by
Viktor & Rolf for the
Spring/Summer 1999
collection. (Collection
Groninger Museum;
photographer:
Peter Tahl)

3 This cape by Giles
for the Autumn/Winter
2004 collection uses
shoulder pads to
create a shoulder line
at right angles to
the neck.

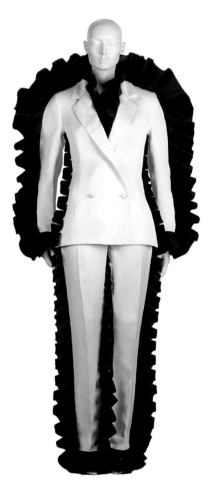

2

3

Choosing the subtleties of silhouette and cut is essential, but some designers choose to make bolder statements by working far more sculpturally on the body. Leigh Bowery was an Australian designer and performance artist who died in 1994. He appeared to be completely unconcerned with convention or perceptions of taste, possibly because he never trained formally in fashion design. Bowery constantly experimented with his own silhouette, augmenting and constricting it, using boning, padding and even gaffer tape. He even displaced his own flesh (hence the gaffer tape) so the line between (temporary) body modification and clothing became blurred. Leigh explains: 'Because I'm chubby I can pleat the flesh across my chest and hold it in place with heavy-grade gaffer tape. Then, by wearing a specially constructed, under-padded bra, I create the impression of a heaving bosom with a six-inch cleavage.' (*Leigh Bowery: The Life and Times of an Icon*, Sue Tilley, page 107)

The clothes would often fit because he altered the shape of his own body. Bowery's body was capable of innumerable shapes and forms. 'The idea of transforming oneself gives courage and vigour. It reduces the absurdity, you can do anything dressed like this. I want to disturb, entertain and stimulate. It's more about silhouette alteration than restriction, though I do like that frisson of sexual danger. I like to think th reform rather than deform the body.' (*Le Bowery: The Life and Times of an Icon*, Tilley, page 112)

1 Australian performance artist, fashion designer and icon, Leigh Bowery. (Photograph Courtesy of Fergus Greer and Perry Rubenstein Gallery)

2 The legacy of Bowery's vision can often be seen in the work of contemporary designers: for example, that of Gareth Pugh. This image is taken from Gareth Pugh's Spring/Summer 2006 collection.

1

For the Comme des Garçons Spring/Summer 1997 collection, down pads were sewn into dresses in irregular places, creating a new silhouette and challenging preconceptions of the body and conventions of beauty by making the wearer look ill-proportioned and deformed.

1

1 Dress by Comme des Garçons for their Spring/Summer 1997 collection.

2 Viktor & Rolf, haute couture Autumn/Winter 1999–2000 collection, First, Second, Third, Fourth, Fifth, Sixth, Seventh, Eighth and Final Preparation.

This series of nine outfits by Dutch designers Viktor & Rolf was inspired in part by the idea of Russian Matryoshka dolls. The smallest outfit was shown on a model and then the next outfit was fitted over the top. This continued until the model was wearing nine outfits, one on top of the other, and each garment augmented the existing silhouette of the previous outfit. (Collection Groninger Museum; Photographer: Peter Tahl)

3 Dress with leather belt by designer Emma Cook for her Spring/ Summer 2006 collection. The belt gives the illusion of a raised waist.

Dutch designers Viktor & Rolf explore the sculptural potential of silhouette. Their clothes often parody recognisable forms, historical references and traditional haute couture, but with fresh vision and humour. Scale and volume are taken to extremes, and in so doing they display their mastery over construction and tailoring and an understanding of the symbolic value of clothing.

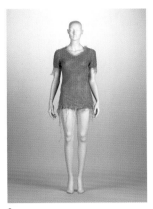  

2

3

Proportion and line

The proportions of a garment develop from the silhouette. If the silhouette is the overall shape of the garment then proportion is how the body is divided up either through lines (horizontal, vertical, diagonal or curved) or with blocks of colour or fabric. Every time we shop for clothes or get dressed we are playing with the perceptions of our own proportions. How and where we break up our bodies with horizontal hem lines, trouser widths, necklines and the position and emphasis of the waist depends on what flatters us.

The line of the garment generally refers to its cut; where seams and darts are placed on the body and the effect they have visually. Confusingly, some designers will refer to the line of a garment when they actually mean silhouette.

The important thing to remember about any lines that are created on clothes is that they must be judged visually and balanced against each other and any other details – for example, openings, necklines and pockets in the vicinity.

General rules

- Vertical lines lengthen the body.
- Horizontal lines emphasise width.
- Straight lines are perceived to be hard and masculine.
- Curved lines are considered to be soft and feminine.
- Seams and darts are not standard and can be moved around the body.
- Garments can be of any length, creating horizontal lines across the body.
- Layers of clothing create multiple lines.

1 The curved seams of this Balenciaga outfit from Spring/Summer 2004 give the impression of an hourglass silhouette.

2 This Lanvin dress from Autumn/Winter 2006 creates a trompe-l'oeil silhouette using line and blocks of colour.

3 The white lines of the seams, darts and edges of this Chanel jacket from Autumn/Winter 2005 exaggerate the effect such lines have on the body. The darts in particular help to suggest a narrow waist.

1

2

God is in the details

An outfit can have a dramatic silhouette and good line, but without great detailing it can seem amateur and unresolved. Outfits that lack detail can survive on the catwalk, but will not bear close scrutiny – for example, on the rail in a shop. Details in clothes are often the clincher when it comes to persuading someone to part with their money. Detailing is particularly important in menswear, where outlandish silhouette, line, fabric and pattern are off-putting to what is a largely conservative clientele.

Details are practical considerations: which fastening to choose, which type of pocket to have and how much topstitching to use. Clever use of detail can also be used to give a collection of clothes a unique identity, a signature; cutting a pocket in a particular way, using an embellishment in one area of a garment or the finishing of an edge can help to differentiate the garments of one designer from those of another.

Pocket types and fastenings can sound a little mundane, but choosing these things doesn't have to be like shopping for items from a catalogue. Although a pocket, for example, has a generic function, and the concept is fixed, it doesn't mean that how it is conceived has to be formulaic. There are rules about how certain pockets are made and how certain pockets look, but these notions can be distorted and reinvented. Fashion rules are made to be broken.

1

1   Magician Coat by British designers Boudicca for the Autumn/Winter 2005 collection. The front has a 'fake' rever collar that is seamed in. The cuffs are 'striped' with top-stitching, as are the small circular panels on the shoulders. The line of the fringed circle gives the effect of epaulettes.

2   Explode Pocket shirt and Pocket One jacket, Spring/Summer 2005, and Simulation skirt, Autumn/Winter 2005, all by Boudicca. Both shirt and jacket have suspended pockets. The shirt has an 'exploding' collar and the jacket has multiple vents at the back of the sleeves.

2

Fabric, colour and texture

You must understand the different varieties and qualities of fabric before you can apply them to a design. If the fabric is already in front of you, then knowing what you can design with it is paramount. For example, chiffon won't make a tailored jacket as well as a wool fabric, and leather does not drape well.

Fabric choices are often dictated by your theme and season. Your theme may suggest a mood or colour palette that can then be interpreted into fabric. The season you are designing for directs the weights, and, to a degree, the textures. Lighter fabrics tend to be used more in Spring/Summer collections and heavier fabrics, suitable for outerwear, tend to be used more for Autumn/Winter. Season can also influence colour. Lighter colours are often used more in Spring/Summer and darker tones for Autumn/Winter. The feel and drape of a fabric will guide you as to what type of garment you can make with it – and this familiarity will buy you experience.

The way you choose to use colour is generally an issue of personal taste and there are few rules, although some combinations should generally be avoided. Red and black together can look clichéd. Traditionally, black and navy should not be worn together, but this is no longer a hard-and-fast rule. Too many primary colours can look garish or cheap, though in the right hands it can work, often by complementing them with a more subdued colour. Some colours don't work next to certain skin tones. Beige and other 'flesh' tones can make skin look pink or red. Using a small amount of a colour as a highlight or accent when contrasted with other colours can have a stronger impact than using large blocks of competing colour.

1

1   Dresses by Vinti Andrews.

2   Scarf by Missoni.

3   The Italian company Missoni is known for its knitwear. Here, pastel colours are balanced by the use of neutral and dark tones.

" *I try to draw from day to day. Things I find and things I see...I'm trying to define a style that has nothing to do with fashion; it's more about individuality.* "

Jens Laugesen talking to Alexander McQueen

2

3

Each season tends to highlight specific fashionable colours. Trend forecasters predict which colours will be prevalent by analysing catwalk shows and making an overview of that season's most popular colours. Some colours are enduring, however. Black tends to be constantly in fashion as it is slimming and can easily be worn with other colours. Certain colour palettes become synonymous with certain designers. For example, Helmut Lang and Jil Sander typically use blacks, greys, muted colours and neutrals. Designers also make use of certain patterns as part of their signature. Paul Smith has become associated with a certain candy-stripe pattern and Missoni is known for its knitted zigzag.

You should develop a range of colours and fabrics when designing. Any initial colour and fabric choices might need building on to fill in gaps. For example, a choice of five colours or fabrics may need an additional two to make the palette flow. Initial fabric choices may not have the breadth of weights and textures necessary to design a variety of clothing.

1

1 This outfit by Anne Valerie Hash for Spring/Summer 2006 breaks up the body into distinct blocks of colour. The proportional use of colour makes the top half of the body appear smaller in comparison to the bottom half.

2 An initial range of fabrics has been collected in this research book by Benjamin Kirchhoff.

' Some people focus on retro, meaning sixties and seventies revivals. Some people stick to very traditional classic clothing, what we call "real" clothes, very easy to put on, simple clothes. I wanted to create something that didn't belong to any of those categories, and go forward. '

Rei Kawakubo, the weekend *Guardian* magazine 1st March 1997

2

Rendering your ideas

Drawing is a tool with which to communicate your design ideas – literally, getting what's in your head on to paper. Ideas can be worked out three-dimensionally on the stand, but even this method of designing requires development on paper at some stage.

It is not essential to be great at drawing to be a good designer, but it helps. Drawing can be an intimidating activity, especially if you're out of practice. The thing to remember is that unless you plan on being a fashion illustrator, it is the design that is most important, not the drawing. Practice and repetition is the key to improving drawing skills, though the repetition itself should be thoroughly interrogated; a bad habit or mannerism can become automatic if you are not actively thinking about what is being rendered; a claw shape where the hand should be becomes less hand-like the more you lose your objectivity.

As a designer working primarily with the body, it would be useful for you to undertake some life-drawing classes at some stage. Drawing the naked human body will help you to understand anatomy, musculature and proportion, as well as how the body works in terms of balance and stance. Drawing a dressed form is useful, too, in order to understand how clothes work on the body. Both exercises require you to use art media and to experiment with mark-making. Incidentally, 'mark-making' means how the art materials are used to put ideas down on paper.

1

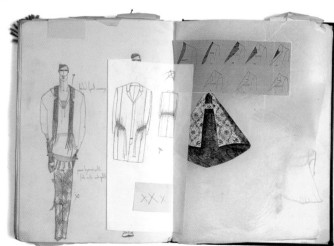

1/2 Examples of fashion
drawings found in
student sketchbooks.

Fashion drawing versus fashion illustration

It is useful to make a distinction between fashion drawing and fashion illustration. A fashion illustration is not so much about the design, but about capturing the spirit of the clothes. Illustration can be used to express a mood or give the clothes context by setting a scene where the clothes might be worn or representing the kind of person who might wear the clothes through styling, make up, hair and pose. A fashion illustration does not need to show the whole of a garment unless it is used in a portfolio in which a design has not been made up into a real outfit or garment. With the latter, the illustration takes the place of a photograph, showing how the garment would look on the body.

Mark-making and the use of varied art materials is much more important in fashion illustration than in design. The best mark-making is that which is confident, fluid and full of movement, and this is something you can develop over time. Use multimedia art materials for more layered, interesting images. Different types of art materials can also help to express different textures of fabric.

A fashion drawing is about communicating your design ideas, although it can also be about capturing the spirit of the clothes. A fashion drawing is a figurative form that is used to get ideas down quickly. It doesn't need to be fancy or the best drawing you have ever done. What it does need to be is fairly proportional; it has to bare a convincing resemblance to a 'real' human form. If the proportions of your drawing are too abnormal this will follow through to the proportions of your designs; what looks good on a figure that has too-long legs won't necessarily look good on a real person. Although anything looks good on someone with long legs, which is why long legs work well on the catwalk.

A fashion drawing also needs to be a fairly fast drawing; in an ideal world, when the creative juices are flowing, ideas come to you rapidly and need to be put down on paper quickly before they are forgotten. And forgotten they will be, because the mind has a habit of moving on to other ideas. As you draw your designs, try to put down colour and fabric as often as possible; your designs are not only about silhouette and detail, but about colour and fabric, too.

Fashion drawing and illustration are not solely about rendering the human form in a realistic manner. Some fashion drawings are so stylised they seem to rely little on a real human figure, rather they rely on a knowledge of fashion drawing itself (in other words, referencing other fashion drawings) and some fashion drawings become more like cartoons. With practice, your fashion drawing will eventually take on a character of its own and become as individual as your signature.

2

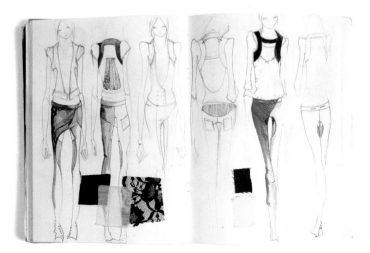

'Fashion illustration is as exciting and expressive as each illustrator's individual artistic interpretation of a designer's idea. Whether it is an illustrator's decision to focus on the detail, the silhouette, a narrative story or the flourish of a quick sketch of the design being drawn, it can be something which captures the spirit of a collection with the signature of another artist's eye and hand. As technology develops, the fashion illustrator has the choice to work with the purity of craft: pencil, pen, paintbrush, crayon, biro, collage, paint, airbrush, ink, or computer artistry – or to combine the two. The choice of focus and technique is as unlimited as an illustrator's imagination. The uses of fashion illustration can vary from the freedom of the illustrator's personal response in editorial work to the specific directions suggested by a creative brief. If the illustration is to be used within a commercial capacity, for example a fashion designer's marketing, advertising or packaging, it can be a way of developing a corporate identity with the flair of artistic expression. '

Richard Gray, fashion illustrator

1

1 Fashion illustration   3 Examples
  by Richard Gray   of templates.

2 Working drawing of
  a motorcycle jacket.

Templates

Design drawing is about speed; getting your ideas on to paper as quickly as possible before you forget them. If you are a beginner, you can use templates of pre-drawn figures which can then be traced through layout paper (or any other transparent paper), speeding up the process of designing. Templates can be found in 'How to do Fashion Illustration/Drawing' books or can be developed from your own drawings. It is preferable to develop templates from your own drawings to keep them individual. But, be warned: if you rely too much on templates it will mean that your freehand fashion drawing will suffer through lack of practice.

Working drawings

When drawing designs, you might include little artistic flourishes that have little to do with the design, but are more to do with mark-making or how you imagine the fabric to fold and move. You may also have unresolved issues, such as fastenings, topstitching, seams, darts, etc., and these issues need to be addressed at some point. This can take place during pattern-cutting and making the toile, but if someone else is going to cut the pattern for the garment these issues need to be addressed sooner rather than later.

Working drawings – also called technical drawings, specifications ('specs') or 'flats' – are flat drawings of the garment, front and back, as if the garment is laid out on a table, showing all its details and accurate proportions. Working drawings are line drawings only; they are purely about structure and detail. Many are executed with a black fine-line pen. One pen (for example, 0.8mm width) may be used for outline, seams, darts and details (depending on what they are) and a finer pen (for example, 0.3mm width) can be used for topstitching.

There are two methods of representing topstitching: as a continuous fine line, which, in fact, it is, or more commonly as a dotted or dashed line. If using the latter method make sure that the dots or dashes are neat, regular and dense or it gives the appearance of large, crude hand-tacking stitches.

You may also use a fine line for buttons, press-studs or other details; there is no one rule, and as long as you are communicating the garment accurately there should not be any problem.

In industry, the drawings are given to a pattern cutter so that he or she can cut the pattern for the design. The drawings should communicate the design accurately so that the pattern cutter doesn't have to second-guess any aspect, so they must be well thought-through. Working drawings are also useful for the sample machinist to help with construction when there is no toile available.

2

3

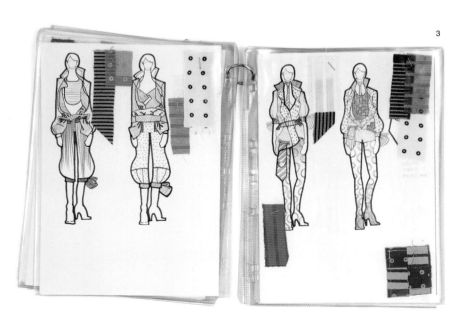

Which media?

Designing on paper is about communication. Colour and fabric are integral to the design, so the more accurately they are represented the more successful the rendering of the design. Learning to understand and use at least one type of paint is very useful; this will enable you to mix colours to gain the most accurate effects. Speed can also be a factor in your choice of art media; coloured pencils and marker pens are by far the easiest to use in terms of translating an idea on to the page.

Each designer has a favoured choice of art material, but don't decide too early on without trying out as many different kinds as possible. Experimentation is the key and using different combinations of materials can yield interesting effects. The following list includes some of the art materials commonly employed for design work. It is not definite, but should provide you with a good starting point.

Paintbrushes (1)

Only use good quality ones made from sable or other natural hairs; cheaper brushes start to 'flare' very quickly making neat painting difficult. When cleaning your brushes use soap to get all residue of paint out of the hairs – and never leave a paint brush standing in a glass of water or the hairs will bend permanently.

Magic markers (2)

Superior-quality felt tips, but without the scratchy marks that are characteristic of cheap felt-tip pens. The colour dries flat, and once dry can be given subsequent layers for a slightly darker tone.

Fine-line pens (3)

These are used for working drawings, but can also be employed to put an outline around a fashion drawing.

Clutch pencil and lead (4/5)

Using a clutch pencil is preferable to a normal pencil because the lead is always fine. The leads are graded according to how relatively soft or hard they are. For example, H leads are hard and B leads are soft. HB falls somewhere in between. For design drawing, leads between HB and 3B are preferable. For pattern-cutting a harder lead, between HB and 3H is best.

Pencil sharpener (6)

Used to sharpen normal pencils to achieve a fine point.

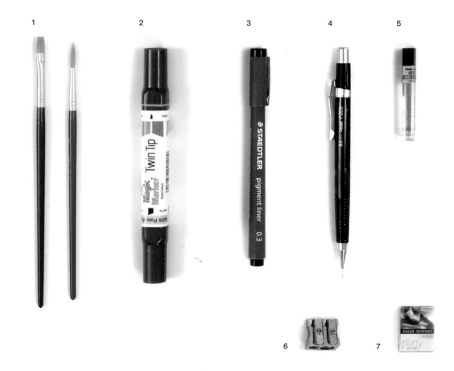

9   10   11   12

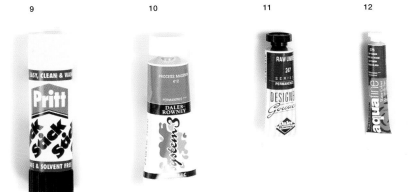

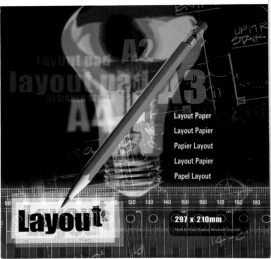

13

Putty rubber (7)

This is a good eraser for getting rid of pencil smudges and grubby fingerprints. It can also be moulded into a fine point and is therefore more controllable than hard erasers.

Water-soluble colouring pencils (8)

These are quick and easy to use as long as you don't insist upon colouring everything in heavily as this will make your wrist ache and your pencil shrink! It is a tonal art medium. Water-soluble coloured pencils behave like a (slightly inferior) watercolour when water is applied by brush.

Adhesive glue stick (9)

Adhesive glue sticks are drier than most glues which stops paper from buckling. Another advantage is that if something is stuck down and you want to reposition it, the glue is tacky enough to enable you to do so.

Acrylic paint (10)

Unlike gouache, acrylic paint does not dry flat; it retains brush marks and texture.

Gouache paint (11)

This is an opaque paint that should be mixed to the consistency of yoghurt. Its opacity allows for lighter colours to be painted on top once the original layer is dry. It has a matt, slightly chalky finish and dries a shade or two lighter than wet. It can be used tonally, moving from light to dark (and back again) by watering it down, but is more commonly used to 'block in' colour of one tone.

Watercolour paint (12)

A transparent paint, generally used on watercolour paper – a heavy, textured cartridge paper. Because watercolour paint is transparent if it is used on any paper other than white, the paper colour has a tendency to show through, effectively mixing the paint with the colour of the paper beneath. Watercolour is used tonally and the intensity of colour is directed by how much it is diluted with water. With watercolours, your aim is a fluid technique, so keep the brush wet and learn to work quickly.

Layout paper (13)

Slightly transparent paper that is used in conjunction with templates. It is not recommended if you want to use an art medium that requires water as the paper is too fine and will buckle.

Portfolios

The graduate portfolio

The result of each assessment during, and upon completion, of a fashion degree course is a portfolio of work. Together with research sketchbooks, this is what you show to prospective investors, employers, stylists and journalists in order to pique their interest.

Your graduation portfolio will include fashion drawings, fashion illustrations, working drawings, fabric swatches, mood-boards, fabric-boards, photographs of actual garments and outfits. There might also be samples of details, including examples of embroidery or a particular method of finishing a garment.

1

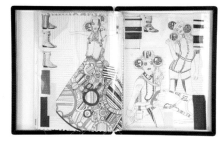

1. Examples of student portfolios.

2. Portfolios can also be specially made. This one is made from layers of acrylic and the surface has been etched into.

3. Pages from UK designers Boudicca's press portfolio, where press is collected and used as a promotional tool.

An independent designer's portfolio

As an independent designer, your portfolio will eventually become much more about recording the clothes and the collections you have made. There may be catwalk shots or the results of a shoot styled by you or with a stylist of your collection. The portfolio also becomes an archive for your press cuttings.

An industry portfolio

As a professional designer working for other companies your portfolio will feature work you have designed for your employers, including photos and sketches, as well as press reviews of your design work. Most of the design drawing that you do if you are working for a company will be executed as working drawings, so it is essential that you include evidence of this in the portfolio.

These last two examples of portfolios are very different in content and focus from the graduate portfolio. While they represent a more professional body of work, this does not negate the importance of the graduate portfolio, which is the designer's first step towards a professional approach to a career in fashion design.

2

3

FABRICS AND TECHNIQUES

As a fashion designer you must have an understanding of fabrics and what their properties are. For example, how fabrics are constructed, what they are made from and how they perform. This knowledge will allow you to choose the right fabric for your designs.

It is also important to be aware of the various techniques that can be applied to your chosen fabric. This will give you endless possibilities to your designs; for example, a fabric could be dyed or printed to add extra colour, embellished, embroidered or pleated to give surface interest. Try to learn as many fabric names and techniques as possible, in this way you will be able to communicate your fabric ideas easily to others.

2

Fabric

It is of fundamental importance for every designer to understand the properties and qualities of fabrics. The choice of fabric for a garment is paramount to its success. Firstly, the weight and handle of a fabric will affect the silhouette of a garment, giving it shape and form or allowing it to drape; for example, silk will have more of a 'draping' quality than heavy wool, which will have more structure. Secondly, a fabric will be chosen for its performance in relation to its function; for example, jeans must be comfortable, durable and long-lasting – and denim is the perfect fabric for this. A raincoat must ideally be lightweight, but still offer protection from the elements; a Teflon-coated cotton would be ideal for this kind of garment. A tight-fitting T-shirt would be best made in a stretchy, breathable fabric, possibly 100% cotton-knitted jersey. Finally, fabrics must be chosen for their aesthetic value; in other words, the way they look and feel, their colour, pattern or texture.

Let's look a little more closely at the defining characteristics of fabrics. What is the composition of a fabric? Are the fibres derived from natural or man-made sources? How is the fabric constructed? Is it for example knitted, woven or maybe crocheted?

1

1/2 From *Wonderland* magazine, Sept/Oct 2005. (Photographer: Kent Baker)

❛ *Fashion is what one wears oneself. What is unfashionable is what other people wear.* ❜

Oscar Wilde (from a book of his quotes)

2

Natural fibres

1

1 Top row from left to right: Fur, leather, woven fabrics: wool, 50 per cent hemp 50 per cent cotton, raw silk, cotton. Bottom row from left to right: Knitted: wool, cotton, silk, linen, printed silk.

2 Jessica Ogden printed Indian cotton dress, Spring/Summer 2006 collection.

2

Natural fibres are derived from organic sources; these can be divided into plant sources (in other words, those composed of cellulose) or animal sources (those composed of protein).

Cellulose fibres

Cellulose is made of carbohydrate and forms the main part of plant cell walls. It can be extracted from a variety of plant forms to make fibres suitable for textile production. Here we are looking at fabrics that are most suitable for the production of garments; they must be soft enough to wear and not break up when worn or washed.

Cotton is a prime example of a plant fibre; it has a soft, 'fluffy' character and grows around the seed of the cotton plant; these fibres are harvested from the plant, processed and spun into cotton thread. Cotton fibres are used to produce 40 per cent of the world's textiles. Its enduring popularity is its extreme versatility; it can be woven or knitted into a variety of weights. It is durable and has breathable properties, which is useful in hot climates as it absorbs moisture and dries off easily.

With most cotton production, farmers have used chemical fertilisers and pesticides on the soil and sprayed them on the plants in order to prevent disease, improve the soil and to increase their harvest. The chemicals are absorbed by the cotton plant and remain in the cotton during manufacture, which means that it is still in the fabric that we wear next to our skin. Due to environmental issues, manufacturers are increasingly developing organic fibres that are grown and processed without the use of artificial fertilisers and pesticides.

Organic fabric production is more expensive, but it has a low impact on the environment and is healthier for the consumer. Designers pursuing organic solutions are Katherine Hamnett and Edun.

Linen has similar properties to cotton, especially in the way it handles, although it tends to crease more easily. It is produced from the flax plant and is commonly regarded as the most ancient fibre. Hemp, ramie and sisal are also used to produce fabrics as an alternative to cotton.

1 Examples of animals that natural fibres originate from: llamas, a merino sheep, and an angora goat.

2 Wildlifeworks womens wear collection, Spring/Summer, 2006. Wildlifeworks collections are made from organic fabrics and are produced in their fair-trade factory in Kenya. (Photographer: Rama)

Protein fibres

Protein is essential to the structure and function of all living cells. The protein fibre 'keratin' comes from hair fibres and is the most commonly used protein fibre in textile production.

Sheep produce wool fleece on their skin for protection against the elements and this can be shorn at certain times of the year and spun into wool yarn. Different breeds of sheep produce different qualities of yarn. Wool has a warm, slightly elastic quality, but it doesn't react well to excessive temperatures; when washed in hot water it shrinks due to the shortening of fibres. Goats are also used to produce wool; certain breeds produce cashmere and angora. Alpaca, camel and rabbit are all also used to produce fabrics with a warm, luxurious quality.

1

2

3 Winni Lok angora
   mohair jumper.

4 Jean-Paul Gaultier
   dress with silk frill,
   originally shown in

i-D magazine, October
2005. (Photographer:
Nick Knight.
Photograph ©
Nick Knight)

Silk is derived from a protein fibre and is harvested from the cocoon of the silkworm. The cocoon is made from a continuous thread that is produced by the silkworm as it wraps it around itself for protection. Cultivated silk is stronger and has a finer appearance than silk harvested in the wild. During the production of cultivated silk the lava is killed, enabling the worker to collect the silk and unravel it in a continuous thread. In the wild, the silkworm chews its way out of its cocoon, thereby cutting into what would otherwise be a continuous thread.

3

4

Man-made fibres

Man-made fibres are made from cellulosic and non-cellulosic fibres. Cellulose is extracted from plants, especially trees. Man-made fibres such as rayon, Tencel, acetate, triacitate and Lyocell are cellulosic fibres as they contain natural cellulose. All other man-made fibres are non-cellulosic, which means they are made entirely from chemicals and are commonly known as synthetics.

Developments in the chemical industry in the 20th century caused a transformation in fabric production. Chemicals that had previously been used for textile finishing techniques began to be used to extract fibres from natural sources to make new fibres.

Rayon was one of the first man-made fabrics to be developed. It is extracted from cellulose and was developed to mimic the qualities of silk; to be strong, absorbent, to drape well and have a soft handle. Different chemicals and processes are used in the production of rayon, each with its own name; these include acetate rayon, cuprammonium rayon and viscose rayon, which is known commonly as viscose. Lyocell and modal are evolved from rayon.

Tencel was developed to be the first environmentally friendly man-made fabric. It is made from sustainable wood plantations and the solvent used to extract it can be recycled. It is a strong fabric that drapes like silk, with a soft handle.

1   Top row: fabrics include cotton/nylon/lycra mix, nylon, nylon ripstop, poly-cotton, Teflon-coated poly-cotton, polyester/wool/mohair mix. Bottom row: fabrics include mohair/cotton/viscose mix, polyester, poly-cotton, nylon mesh, polyester.

2   Liberty & Co. evening coat, c1925. The coat is made from silk rayon jacquard and has a gold chrysanthemum pattern. The cuffs and hems are gold rayon and the collar is made from beaver fur. This is an example of an early use of rayon in womenswear. (Liberty of London, Evening Coat, c1925. Collection of the Kyoto Costume Institute, Photograph by Richard Haughton)

Synthetic fibres

Germany was the centre of the chemical industry until after the First World War when the USA took over their chemical patents and developed their inventions. DuPont was one of the large chemical companies developing fabrics at this time. In 1934, DuPont was able to produce long polymeric chains of molecules, the first being the polymer nylon. This was the beginning of the developments of synthetic fabrics.

Nylon is a strong, lightweight fibre, but it melts easily at high temperatures. It is also a smooth fibre, which means dirt cannot cling easily to its surface. During the Second World War silk supplies from Japan were cut off, so the US government redirected the use of nylon in the manufacture of hosiery and lingerie to parachutes and tents for the military.

There are several other synthetic fabrics. Acrylic has the look and handle of wool. It is non-allergenic, but melts easily under heat. DuPont developed it in the 1940s. Lastex is an elastic fibre, but after repeated washing loses this quality. It is used in Spandex, which is a super-stretch fibre. Polyester is a strong, crease-resistant fibre developed in 1941 by ICI. It can be recycled from clear, plastic drink bottles. Acetate has the look, but not the handle, of silk. It does not absorb moisture well, but is fast to dry.

1

2

1   Comme des Garçons jacket made from 100 per cent nylon fabric.

2   Stella McCartney for Adidas collection, Spring/Summer, 2006. (Photographer: Alexander Gnädinger for Adidas)

3   Stockings were in short supply during the Second World War as nylon was being used to produce parachutes and tents. In this image, women flock to get sub-standard artificial silk stockings. (Getty Images/Hulton Archive)

Synthetic fibres are best blended with natural fibres to improve their qualities; for example, polyester mixed with cotton will produce a fabric with a natural handle that creases less. Lycra and Spandex can be mixed with other fibres to give a stretch quality so that a fabric retains its shape with wear. It is especially suitable for performance sportswear.

3

Developments in fabric

Many modern developments in fabric have come from research into military use or space travel. For example, the Gore-Tex® brand was first developed as light, efficient insulation for wire on Neil Armstrong's early space mission. It was then developed and registered as a breathable, waterproof and windproof fabric in 1978, and used in the astronauts' suits in the NASA mission in 1981. It is now used widely for its properties in outerwear and sportswear.

Developments also come from looking at nature. Spider silk is naturally stronger than steel, and is stretchy and waterproof. Biochemists are currently studying its structure and developing synthesised fibres with the same properties that could be used for fabric production.

1

Yarn production

During fibre-production man-made fibres are put through a spinning process in which they are forced through small holes in a showerhead-style structure, creating long, continuous fibres called 'filament' fibres. Unlike natural fibres, manufacturers can control the thickness of the fibre, which is called the 'denier'.

Staple fibres are short, natural fibres; an exception to this being silk, which naturally develops in a continuous length. Filament fibres can be cut to resemble staple fibres to mimic the properties of natural fibres. Synthetic fibres are cut down to become staple fibres when they are blended with natural fibres.

After spinning, the fibres are twisted together to form yarn. Yarn can be twisted in various ways to produce different effects in the finished fabric. Crêpe yarn is highly twisted, producing a crinkled surface in the finished fabric. A bouclé yarn has an irregular pattern of loops, or curls, along its length; fabric made from this yarn has a characteristically knobbly surface.

1 Y-3 Spring/Summer 2006 collection sees the use of modern developments in fabric.

2 Linen loop, wool loop, crêpe, tape, mohair, linen, raw silk, silk, cotton slub, wool slub, chenille.

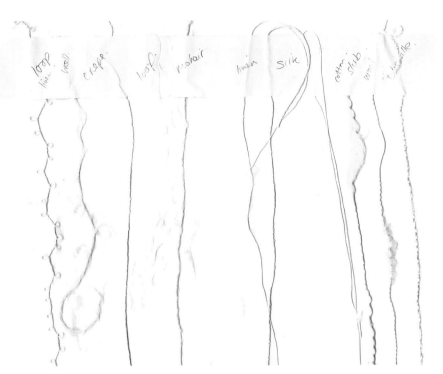

2

" *I think it's important to know your position in the whole fashion discourse and to maintain it, but always add elements that will help you move forward.* "

Hussein Chalayan

Fabric construction

Woven fabrics

A woven fabric is made from a warp that runs down the length of a fabric and a weft that weaves across the breadth of the fabric. The warp and weft are also known as the 'grain'. The warp is put on the loom before weaving, so that it is already stretched, which gives it more 'give' across the width of the fabric. Garments are normally cut with the major seams running parallel to the lengthwise grain; this helps to control the structure of the garment. The bias is at 45 degrees to the warp or weft. Garments can be cut on the 'bias' or cross, which gives characteristic drape and elasticity to a garment.

Weave construction

The way the warp and weft are woven together produces a variety of fabrics. The three main types of weave construction are plain, twill and satin.

Plain weave is constructed from a warp and weft that is similar in size. During weaving the weft passes over alternate warp threads to create the fabric and it is usually closely woven. Plain weaves include calico, flannel and chiffon, and variations to the plain weave include basket weaves, ribs and cords. Basket weave is achieved by alternately passing a weft under and over a group of warp.

With twill weave the weft is woven over at least two warp threads before it goes under one or more warp threads; where this is staggered down the length of the fabric it produces a diagonal weave effect. Gabardines, drills, denims, tweeds and herringbones are good examples of twill weave.

Satin weave has visible sheen and feels smooth; this is due to yarn laying across the surface of the fabric. The warp is woven to lie on top of the weft or vice versa.

Variations on the three basic weave structures include:

Pile fabrics: These are woven with yarns that are 'looped' during weaving; they can then be cut, which is characteristic of corduroy, or left as loops – for example, with towelling.

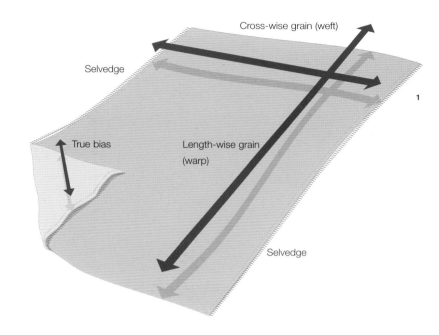

Cross-wise grain (weft)

Selvedge

True bias

Length-wise grain (warp)

Selvedge

1

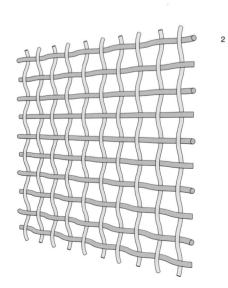

2

1 This diagram illustrates the warp and weft, or 'grain', in fabric.

2 This illustration shows the basic weave structure.

3 From the top, left to right: Wool herringbone, polyester satin, plain cotton. Silk satin, jacquard, silk organza. Cotton velvet, double cloth wool, denim. Cotton rib, wool twill, silk chiffon. All on a corduroy background.

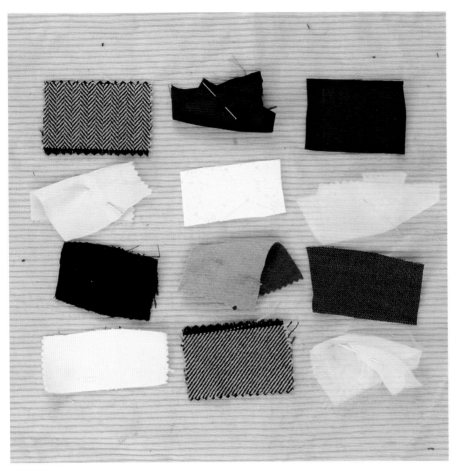

3

Double cloth: This is the result of weaving two interconnected cloths at the same time. Velvet is commonly woven as a double cloth – that is, cut apart after weaving to produce two fabrics that are the same. Double cloth construction can also produce a fabric made of two quite different qualities. This kind of fabric is reversible so that either side can be used as the outer layer of a garment.

Jacquard weaving: This is a complicated weave system in which warp and weft threads are lifted or left to produce patterns and textures. Jacquard weaving includes brocade and damask constructions.

Wrong and right sides

Most fabrics have a front (or 'right') and a back (or 'wrong') side, the front being the side that is usually cut to be visible on the outside of the garment. The 'selvedge' is the edge of the fabric running down the length or warp so that it does not fray.

Knitted fabrics

Knitted fabrics are constructed from interconnecting loops of lengths of yarn, which can be knitted along the warp or weft, giving the fabric its stretchy quality. Horizontal rows of knit are known as 'courses' and vertical rows as 'wales'. Weft knitting is created from one yarn that loops and links along the course; if a stitch is dropped the knit is likely to ladder and run down the length of the wale. Hand-knitting is a prime example. Warp knitting is more like weaving; the construction is more complicated and the fabric is less easy to unravel.

Originally, knitting was produced by hand, but for many years it has been made by machine for mass production. The yarn can be knitted flat as a length of fabric or circular, producing a long tube that can be fashioned to fit – knitted socks are an example of fully fashioned machine knitting. Different thicknesses of knitting can be produced according to the size of the needles and the thickness or the count of the yarn. The number of needles per inch or centimetre of construction is known as the 'gauge'.

1   Jens Laugesen
    upside-down
    sweatshirting bomber
    jacket from the
    Autumn/Winter
    2004 collection.
    (Photographer:
    Jean-Francois Carly)

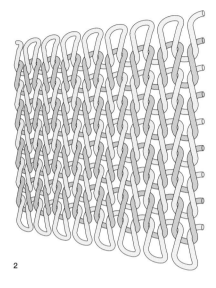

2

Knitting techniques: machine knit and hand knit

Single jersey knit has a front 'knit' and a back 'purl' and is produced when using one bed of needles. Interlock knit or double jersey is produced with a double row of needles and the knit looks the same front and back both showing a knit stitch. Sweatshirting is a heavier knit, the back of which is looped. The loops can be left looped or brushed to achieve a fleece back. Ribs and other textured knitting are produced using two beds of needles knitting alternate knit and purl stitches. Ribs can be used to finish garments on the cuffs or waistband where a garment needs to be gathered in; they have a greater stretch due to their construction. Rib can also be used to produce a whole garment.

2   An illustration showing basic knit structure.

3   Running from top to bottom, machine-knitted fabrics: interlock (showing knit stitch front and back), loop back sweatshirting, rib (showing alternate grouped knit and purl construction), single jersey (showing knit and purl stitches).

3

In addition to different knitting techniques, texture can be created by knitting with different needles, yarn or stitches; for example, cable. Changing the colour of the yarn within a knitted piece can create pattern. Aran, jacquard, Fair Isle and intarsia are all examples of pattern within knit.

Hand-knitting can produce a variety of weights of fabric and has its own 'home-made' character; it is especially suited to very heavy knits and cables. You can produce really creative hand-knitting by increasing the scale of stitches used and even leaving stitches to deliberately ladder.

Knitwear construction

Knitwear can be constructed in three different ways. First, fabric can be knitted as a length, then the garment pieces cut and sewn together. Second, garment pieces are knitted to shape or fully fashioned, then sewn together to produce a garment. Finally, the garment is knitted in three dimensions with little or no seams.

1

2

1   Walter Van Beirendonck sweater.

2   Winni Lok knitted sweater. The front of the garment uses the front or 'right' side of the knitting and the back of the garment uses the back or 'wrong' side of the knitting.

3   Winni Lok knitwear showing cable stitch and laddering, also rib stitching at the cuff.

3

It's happened...the paper dress!

Seventeen June '66

$1.00 PLUS 25¢ FOR HANDLING

The "Paper Caper" by Scott.
It's here! Outrageously 1966!

Be the first in your world to pop up in one—
and make eyes pop. Wear it for parties.... wear
it for play. Wear it for gags—then give it the
go-by. You're what's happening when you
wear your "Paper Caper."
Clip this coupon—mail it today.

RESEARCH DEPARTMENT

GLAMOUR JUN 1966

SCOTT PAPER COMPANY
BOX 1966-G, PHILADELPHIA, PA. 19105

Please send me_____ Scott "Paper Capers." I enclose $_____
Offer expires Dec. 31, 1966. $1 plus 25¢ handling = $1.25 each dress.

CHECK
YOUR
SIZE

BANDANA			OP-ART		
LARGE	SMALL		LARGE	SMALL	
MEDIUM	PETITE		MEDIUM	PETITE	

(Sizes: Petite 3 to 6, Small 7 to 10, Medium 11 to 14, Large 15 to 18)

NAME_____

ADDRESS_____

CITY_____ STATE_____ ZIP_____

1

1 The 'paper caper' dress was produced by Scott Paper Company in 1966 as a promotional tool, available by mail order. (The D'arcy Collection, Communications Library of University of Illinois)

2 Chloé Spring/Summer 2006 collection.

Non-woven fabrics

Different to woven fabrics, non-woven fabrics are produced by compressing fibres together with the use of heat, friction or chemicals. Examples of this are felt, rubber sheeting and techno fabrics such as Tyvek®. Tyvek® is produced by matting fibres together to make a paper-like fabric. It also has a coating that makes it tear-proof, water-resistant, recyclable and machine-washable. However, non-woven fabrics needn't be man-made. Leather and fur might be considered natural non-woven fabrics, for example.

Non-woven fabrics can be used for fashion garments, but are also used for linings, padding and the interiors of shoes and bags. Due to their construction, non-woven fabrics do not fray or unravel in the same way as woven fabrics.

Other fabrics

Some fabrics cannot be classified as either woven, knitted or non-woven in construction. These include macramé, crochet and lace. Macramé is constructed through the ornamental knotting of yarn, lending the fabric a 'hand-crafted' appearance. Crochet stitches are made using a single hook to pull one or more loops through previous loops of a chain.

This construction is built up to form a patterned fabric. Different to knitting, it is composed entirely of loops made secure only when the free end of the strand is pulled through the final loop. Lace-making produces a fabric that is light and open in structure. The negative holes in lace are as important as the positive stitches in the overall pattern of the fabric.

2

Surface treatments

Once a fabric has been constructed, it can be enhanced or altered with the application of different kinds of surface treatments. Techniques include print, embellishment, dyeing and wash finishes.

1

2

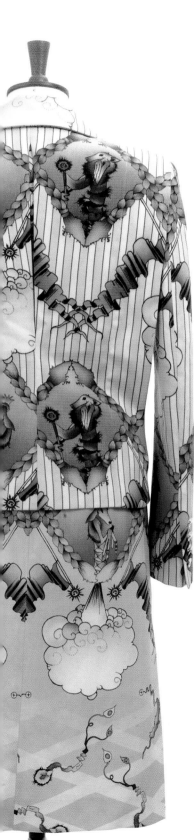

1 Jonathan Saunders Spring/Summer 2006. The colours in the top of this dress are beautifully reflected in the print design in the lower part of it.

2 Prada over-printed dress. Originally shot for *i-D* magazine, October 2005. The dress was first made then printed over; when the body moves, the print separates to show the unprinted fabric in the creases. (Photographer: Nick Knight. Photograph © Nick Knight)

3 Basso & Brooke inkjet print. This print has been generated in the computer.

Print

Pattern, colour and texture can be applied to fabric by printing. Fabric can be printed by various methods, including screen, block, roller, mono, hand or digital printing.

Screen printing requires a design, ink, squeegee and a 'silkscreen' – that is, a piece of silk stretched evenly across a frame. The first step is to make a stencil of the design, which is applied to the screen, blocking the silk so the ink can only pass through the 'positive' areas of the design. The screen is placed on the fabric and the ink is pulled through the screen evenly with the squeegee, leaving a printed image on the fabric. The print is then fixed on to the fabric with heat so that it will not wash off. Multicoloured designs are created by using different screens for different colours.

Block printing is one of the earliest forms of printing. A design is applied to a hard material – for example, wood, lino or rubber – via embossing or by cutting into the surface to make a negative image. This block can then be coated with ink and, with pressure, applied to the fabric to form an imprint.

Roller printing produces a continuous design on a fabric. This is useful for designs with a repeat image over a large print area as this method enables seamless printing so that the joins in the design are invisible.

As the name implies, mono printing produces a single, unique print. Inks are applied to a surface that is then transferred to the fabric, in reverse, to make a print. Hand painting is made directly on to the fabric using one of a number of tools, such as brushes and sponges. Hand painting gives a 'hand-made' feel to a piece of fabric. It can be a slow process for producing a long length of fabric.

Digital printing can be applied directly to fabric from the computer via an inkjet printer. Very high-definition imaging can be achieved, and many colours can be printed without the need for numerous screens. Laser printers are also used, but it is still a relatively expensive process.

3

Printing dyes and agents

To print a colour a dye is used with an oil- or water-based thickening agent, which stops the dye from bleeding in the design. An oil-based ink is more opaque and heavy and tends to sit on the surface of the fabric. It is available in a range of colours and finishes, including pearlescent, metallic or fluorescent. Water-based inks produce fabrics with a better handle as the thickening agent can be washed out after the fabric has been printed and fixed.

A fabric can also undergo 'discharge' printing. First, the fabric must be dyed with a dischargeable colour. The fabric is then printed with a substance that bleaches away (or 'discharges') the dye. Discharge printing is useful if a pale-coloured image is required against a dark background.

In addition to colour, texture can be achieved on fabrics via printing methods. Chemicals can be used to produce a 'relief' effect on the surface of the fabric or to 'eat away' the fabric for surface interest. Expantex is a brand of chemical that when printed and heated, produces an embossed effect on fabric. Fabrics can also be printed with glue then heat-pressed with flock paper. The flock adheres to the glue, giving a raised 'felt' effect. Glitter and foil can be similarly applied to produce special effects. Fabrics constructed with both natural and synthetic fibres within the warp and the weft can be printed with a devoré paste. When heated, the paste burns away one of the fibres, leaving behind a pattern where the other fibre remains.

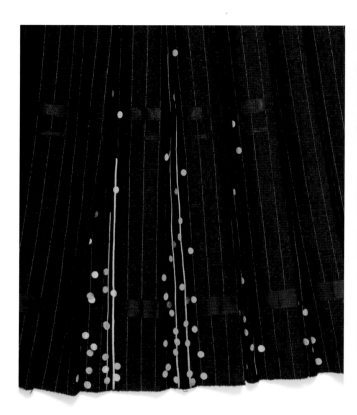

1

Devoré

Devoré is a printing technique that produces a burnt-out image on a fabric that is a mixture of man-made and natural fibres. The devoré paste burns out either the man-made or the natural fibre.

2

1 Jenny Udale pleated oil-based print. The print is applied within the pleats in the skirt so the design is only seen when the pleats open.

2 Jenny Udale pleated devoré print. The fabric was first devoréd, then sunray pleated.

3 Hand-embroidered sweatshirt by Peter Jensen.

4 Hand-embroidered jacket by Jessica Ogden.

Print and design

Designs can be applied in a repeat manner to a length of fabric or as a placement to a specific part of a garment. A design does not necessarily need to be just on the front or back of a garment. It makes for an interesting effect when a printed design works around the body and affects other design elements, such as the placement of seams. In this way, the print is integral to the construction of the garment.

Embellishment

Another way to add surface interest to fabric is to embellish rather than print, which gives a more three-dimensional and decorative look than printing. Techniques for embellishment include embroidery, appliqué, cutwork, beading and fabric manipulation.

Embroidery

Embroidery can be used as an embellishment on the surface of the cloth to enhance the look of the fabric. Contemporary embroidery is based on traditional techniques. Hand stitching is the basis of these, and once you have learnt the principles, you have the foundation for a vast array of techniques. There is enormous scope for developing basic stitches. You can achieve fascinating textures and patterns by working in different threads, changing scale and spacing, working formally, working freely and combining stitches to make new ones. The key is to be as creative and innovative as possible.

Machine embroidery can be worked on domestic or industrial machines. The machines can be used creatively and flexibly to produce a wide range of effects and techniques, from controlled to more freestyle work. As with hand embroidery, the techniques can vary in accordance with the choice of thread and fabric.

Embroidery can be applied before or after the construction of a garment, and concentrated in specific areas or as part of an overall design. Embroidery can be used in a way that makes it integral to the function of the garment, rather than simply as a decorative enhancement. For example, a buttonhole can be created with interesting stitch work and a simple garment can change shape through the application of smocking.

3

4

Beading

Beading is essentially embroidery with beads because each bead is attached to the fabric with a stitch. Beads can be made from glass, plastic, wood, bone, enamel and are available in a variety of shapes and sizes. These include seed beads, bugle beads, sequins, crystals, diamanté and pearls. Beading adds texture to fabric; using glass beads on a garment lends the textile a wonderful, light-reflecting, luxurious quality. French beading is the application of beads stitched with a needle and thread on the front of a fabric. Stretching the fabric over a frame can keep the fabric taut, making beading easier and giving the work a more professional finish. Tambour beading is a technique whereby beads and sequins are applied with a hooked needle and a chain stitch from the back of the fabric. It is a more efficient way to apply beads than French beading.

Appliqué

Appliqué means to stitch one piece of fabric to another for decorative effect. Fabric motifs, such as badges, can be beaded or embroidered first and then appliquéd on to the garment with stitch.

Cutwork

Fabrics can also be enhanced through the use of hand cutwork where areas of the fabric are cut away and stitch is applied to stop the raw edges fraying. Cutwork can also be achieved by the use of a laser. Precise patterns can be achieved with laser cutting. The laser also seals, or melts, the edge of man-made fabric with heat, which stops the fabric from fraying. An 'etched' effect can be achieved by varying the depth of the laser cut into the fabric.

1

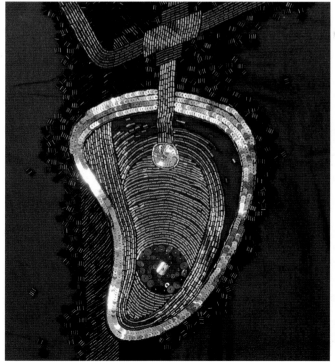

2

1   Richard Sorger
    beaded piece.

2/3 Back of tambour
    beading, showing the
    chain stitch that holds
    down the beads on
    the front of the sample,
    and the tambour hook.

4   Appliqué work in
    Emma Cook's
    Spring/Summer
    2006 collection.

3

4

1   Garment-dyed Preen   2   Advert from Diesel's
    jersey T-shirt.   Autumn/Winter
                             2004 campaign. Diesel
                             uses wash finishes on
                             their denims.

Dyeing

Most fabrics are woven or knitted before they are dyed with synthetic or natural dyes. Natural dyes are derived from plants, animals or minerals. For example, red dyes can be produced from crushed cochineal beetles or the roots of the madder plant. Most natural dyes need a fixative to stop the colour bleeding from the fabric through wear or washing.

Towards the end of the 19th century, fabric manufacture expanded at a rapid pace due to the industrial revolution in Western Europe, predominantly in the UK. Great quantities of natural resources were needed to produce the dyes for the fabric. In some cases, the natural dyes were shipped from abroad, which was expensive and time consuming. As a result, chemists started to look at ways of producing synthetic 'copies' of natural dyes. At this time, a purple dye called Tyrian purple was used to colour cloth used by royalty; it was a difficult and expensive colour to produce as it was extracted from the mucus of molluscs. A young chemist named William Perkin invented the first synthetic purple dye, which was called aniline purple, or mauveine. His discovery made him very wealthy and paved the way for the research and development of other synthetic dyes. Today, synthetic dyes are developed continuously to improve their colourfastness and performance.

Dyeing techniques can be used to create pattern. Two popular methods are resist techniques and tie-dyeing. The latter involves tying fabric in knots before dyeing, which prevents dye from penetrating the cloth in certain areas. When the fabric is untied and dried, undyed areas form a pattern on the fabric. Tie-dyeing has an interesting history. It has been used since ancient times – the Japanese call it 'shibori' – but it was popularised in the West by the craft revival of the 1960s.

Garment dyeing

Fabric is usually dyed in lengths, but it is possible to dye garments after their construction. It is important to first test the cloth for shrinkage; dyeing often requires high temperatures to fix the colour properly, and the heat can cause the fibres to shrink. It is also important that the thread, zips and trims of the garment will react to the dye and not resist the dyeing process.

1

2

4 An example of pleating technique by Issey Miyake.

3

Fabric finishes

Fabric finishes can be applied to a length of fabric or to a garment that has already been constructed. Finishes can alter the look of the fabric; for example, a garment can be stone-washed to produce a pale, faded effect. Finishes can also give the fabric an added function; for example, a fabric can be waterproofed with the addition of a coating of wax.

Wash finishes

Stone-washing was a hugely popular finish in the 1980s and was the fashion style of choice for numerous pop bands of that era. Stone-washing is achieved with the aid of pumice stones, which fades the fabric, but it is difficult to control and can damage the fabric and the machinery used to finish it. Acid dyes were introduced to perform the same task and the effects are called snow or marble washes, but this type of process is not environmentally friendly.

Enzyme washes or bio-stoning are less harmful to the environment. Various effects can be achieved, depending on the mix and quantity of enzyme used within the wash. Enzyme washes can also be used to soften fabrics.

Garments can be sand- or glass-blasted using a gun to target specific areas where fading and distressing is required. Lasers can also be used to produce precisely faded areas on a garment.

Washing or heat can be used to give fabrics a creased or crinkled effect. Fabrics can be randomly creased by washing and leaving them unironed. Creasing and fixing the fabric before washing can form crinkles in specific areas. How long these creases remain in the fabric depends on the process used, the fabric chosen and the heat of the wash; for example, permanent creases can be made on synthetic fabrics through the application of heat, which affects the structure of the fibres.

Aromatic fabrics are created by washing the fabric with a perfume; this is being developed for lingerie. A successful way to fix permanently the smell to the cloth has not yet been developed so the perfume eventually washes out.

Coating finishes

As the term implies, 'coating' finishes are applied to the surface of the fabric.

Fabrics can be waterproofed by applying a layer of rubber, polyvinyl chloride (PVC), polyurethane (PU) or wax over the surface. These fabrics are ideal for outdoor wear and footwear. Teflon-coated fabrics also provide an invisible protective barrier against stains and dirt – useful for practical, easy-clean garments. Breathable waterproof fabric is produced by applying a membrane containing pores big enough to enable perspiration to escape, but small enough to stop moisture droplets to penetrate. Gore-Tex® is a superior example of this kind of fabric and is often used in sportswear. For example, when selecting fabric for a breathable waterproof garment, the fabric properties must be considered. Cotton would allow the body to breathe, but would become damp in the rain. A PU-coated fabric would stop the rain, but retain perspiration against the body. Whereas a fabric such as Gore-Tex® would allow the body to breathe and would also protect from the rain.

Fabric and yarn trade shows

Fabric trade fairs are held biannually in line with the fashion calendar (see page 126). The fairs showcase new developments in fabrics and present samples from manufacturers and the mills. Designers visit these shows for inspiration and to choose fabrics for their designs. Swatch books and fabric hangers are made by the manufacturers and designers select their fabrics from these. Sample lengths of fabrics are then made and sent out to the designer. The designer will then produce the garment samples for a collection and shops will place orders from these. The orders will all be collated and the fabric requirements worked out. The designer will then order the fabric lengths needed for production. If a fabric supplier does not receive enough orders on a fabric, they may not put it into production.

1

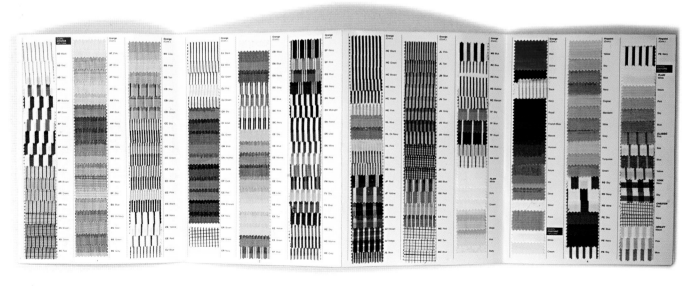

2

1/2 Fabric swatch books 3 Premier Vision 2006.
from which sample
lengths are selected
and ordered.

The main knitting yarn fair is Pitti Filati in Florence and Expofil in Paris. The main fabric fairs are Moda In in Milan, Interstoff in Frankfurt and Premier Vision in Paris. The printed textile fair, Indigo, is held at Premier Vision. Because fabric suppliers must sell fabrics in minimum lengths, it is important to have this in mind when visiting the fairs. For many students, this is simply not realistic. For students who want to buy from the fairs, it is important to check the prices carefully and to find out whether there are hidden costs, such as delivery or supplement fees. Many suppliers will also require a VAT number.

3

CONSTRUCTION

Construction is the foundation of clothing and fashion design. As this chapter demonstrates, it is both a technical and a design issue; garments need seams and darts in order to render a two-dimensional fabric into a three-dimensional piece of clothing, but how and where a designer chooses to construct these lines also affects the proportion and style of a garment. The use of different types of seam is often dictated by the choice of fabric, but can also be design-led; for example, because welt seams (see page 94) are commonly used on denim clothes, they give a garment a workwear feel. A 'deconstructed' seam (a seam shown on the outside) or a raw edge, where appropriate, gives a purposefully 'unfinished' look.

It is important that every fashion designer knows and understands how garments are made. A designer must know, for example, the various possibilities of pocket or collar construction, or where a seam can go. It is only when you know the rules that the rules can be broken to innovative effect.

This chapter introduces you to the basics of construction, taking you through the different types of tools and machinery required and their function in the construction process. It will also look at different sewing techniques, and techniques such as pleating and gathering that are employed to give form, volume and structure in clothing.

Tools and machinery

Before we can talk about the methods for constructing garments, we must look at the array of tools and heavy duty machinery involved in the process of construction. The items that follow are some of the key tools.

Tools

Pattern master (1)

This is used for creating lines, curves and for checking angles.

Tracing wheel (2)

This is used to trace a line from one piece of paper or pattern on to another directly underneath.

Tape measure (3)

You can't begin work as a designer without one of these. It is used for taking measurements of the body. It is also used to measure around curves on a pattern if a pattern master is not available or is too short.

Tailor's chalk (4)

Using tailor's chalk is one way of making lines or transferring a pattern on to cloth.

Pins (5)

Pins are used to temporarily fix pieces of cloth together before they are stitched.

Shears (6)

Large scissors for cutting cloth are referred to as shears. Never use shears to cut paper as this will blunt the blades.

Rotary cutting knife (7)

This circular blade is used to cut fabric. Some people find it easier to cut around a pattern piece with one of these than with shears.

Small pair of scissors, or snips (8)

A pair of these is useful for cutting threads or notches.

Set square (9)

A right-angled triangular plate for drawing lines, particularly at 90 degrees and 45 degrees.

Metre rule (10)

A 100cm ruler useful for drawing long, straight lines.

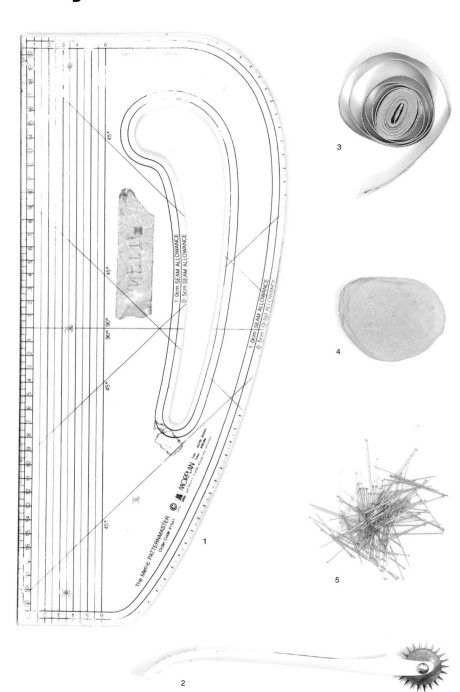

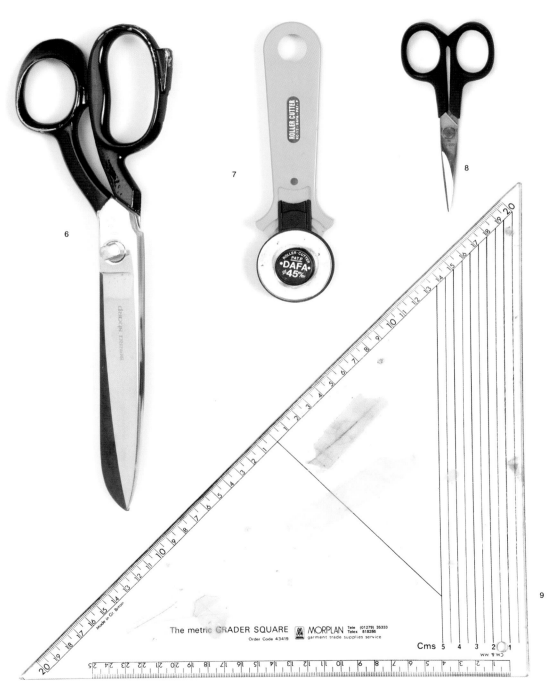

6

7

8

9

10

Machinery

Industrial flat bed machine

This machine does the basic straight stitch used to construct most types of seam. It can sew anything from chiffon to leather, but different types of fabric often require different fittings for the machine and a change in the width of the needle. For example, finer fabrics need finer needles.

Overlocker

An overlocking stitch is a series of threads that combine to create a stitch that literally 'locks' the fabric along its edge, preventing the fabric from fraying. A blade runs along the edge of the fabric, chopping off excess material and threads. Overlocking stitches can be made up of three, four or five threads and the type of fabric dictates which to use.

Overlocking stitch is used in three instances:

1   On woven fabrics to prevent fraying.

2   On knitted stretch fabrics as a method of creating a seam. The overlocking stretches with the fabric and therefore does not break, unlike a running stitch from a flatbed machine, which has no give.

3   A superlock stitch is a dense version of an overlocking stitch and is used on fine fabrics such as chiffon.

Coverstitch

A coverstitch machine is used primarily in the construction and finishing of jersey fabrics and for lingerie. Twin needles create two rows of stitching on the right side of the fabric and an overlocking stitch on the wrong side of the fabric. A variation of this stitch creates an overlocking stitch on both sides of the fabric. Unlike an overlocking machine, this machine does not cut off excess fabric.

1

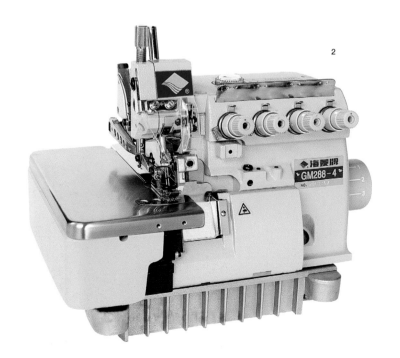

2

1   Industrial flat bed machine.

2   Overlocker.

3   Industrial iron.

4   Fusing press. (Images 1–4 Photographs © J. Braithwaite & Co. Sewing Machines Ltd.)

5   A keyhole buttonhole on a Levi denim jacket.

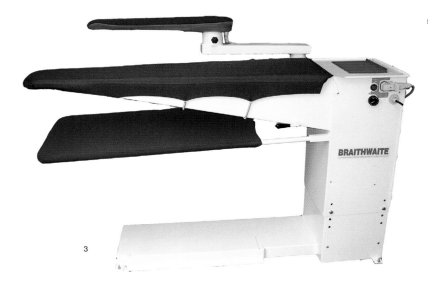

Buttonhole machine

This machine creates two kinds of buttonhole: a 'keyhole' and a 'shirt' buttonhole. Shirt buttonholes are the most common type and are used in most instances where a machine-made buttonhole is desirable. Keyhole buttonholes are mainly used on tailored garments, such as coats and suit jackets.

Industrial iron and vacuum table

An industrial iron, as opposed to a domestic iron, is heavier, more durable and the steam has a higher pressure. It can be used with a vacuum table, which is shaped like an ironing board and often has a smaller board for ironing sleeves attached. A pedal underneath the machine allows the user to create a vacuum while ironing; the air and steam are sucked through the fabric into the bed of the machine. This reduces the steam in the atmosphere and also holds the fabric to the ironing board, allowing for easier pressing.

Pressing is essential to a garment; fabric will crease and rumple as it is handled and manipulated under a machine. Unpressed seams do not lie flat and the garment will look unfinished if it is not ironed.

Fusing press

Fabrics sometimes need more substance and support; for example, cuffs and collars need more body and support than the rest of a shirt.

A fusing press is the industrial machine used to attach (melt) iron-on interfacing to fabric and is more efficient and durable than using an industrial iron.

Construction techniques

Seams

Making a seam is one of the most fundamental skills you will learn as you begin to study construction. A seam is created when two or more pieces of fabric are joined together. 'Seam allowance' is the border around a piece of cloth beyond the stitch line. This extra fabric is allowed in order to create a seam. There are various types of seam and each has a specific use and purpose.

Running seam

This is the most common: two pieces of cloth are joined together using a flat bed machine. The seam allowance is either pressed open or to one side (seam allowance: 10mm+).

French seam

This is so-called because it originated in Paris, the home of haute couture ('high sewing'). This type of seam is used on fine and transparent fabrics to create a neat finish. It involves two rows of stitching; the first is completed on the right side of the fabric and the second line 'traps' the first on the wrong side (inside) of the fabric (seam allowance: 13mm+).

Welt seam

This is the seam commonly used on jeans, jean jackets and other types of denim garments. Two pieces of fabric interlock to form a strong and durable seam. Because of the way the seam is constructed, one side of the fabric will have two rows of stitching and the other side one row (seam allowance: one side 7mm+, the other side 17mm+).

1

2

3

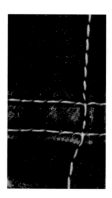

4

5

6

7

1 A Levi's denim jacket constructed using welt seams and topstitching.

2 Running seam with overlocked edges.

3 French seam and pin hem.

4 Welt seam and topstitching.

5 The inside of a Basso & Brooke jacket showing the facing and lining.

6 Ordinary hem.

7 Binding.

8 A Fila sweatshirt screen-printed over with artwork by Dutch designer Bas Kosters. Shows ribbing around the cuffs, collar and hem.

9 Section of a tailored jacket using hand-stitching for construction purposes.

Finishes

Once the seams of a garment have been constructed, the question of how to 'finish' the garment must be addressed. The finish of the garment is exactly that: the completion and tidying of raw edges, necklines, hems and cuffs, and whether to use topstitching or not. How one finishes the garment affects the overall style of the garment and the choice of the finish is an important element of its design.

Topstitching

Any stitching visible on the right side of a garment is referred to as top stitching. It can be decorative, but its main function is to reinforce a seam.

Ordinary hem

An ordinary hem is an allowance of fabric that enables the hem to turn up either once or twice to finish a garment (for example, a hem with a finished depth of 1cm will have 2cm fabric allowance if it is turned up twice). Hems at the bottom of trousers, skirts, dresses and coats are deeper (at least 3cm finished depth).

Pin hem

A pin hem is a very short turned-up hem used to finish fine fabrics, such as chiffon or silk. These are either sewn by machine or by hand.

Facings

A facing is used to finish edges, such as necklines or front/back openings. It looks better than turning the fabric in on itself and stitching it down and allows the finish of a garment to be without topstitching. A facing is usually cut from the same cloth as the outside layer.

Hand sewing

There are various techniques and stitches used in hand sewing. Both tailoring and haute couture employ a wide range of hand stitching in the construction and completion of garments. Each type of stitch has a specific role, whether it is used for hems or attaching canvas to a jacket front.

Binding

A binding is a bias strip of fabric or jersey used to neaten a raw edge. It can be used at necklines, cuffs and hems, but also as a method of neatening the raw edges of an internal seam when overlocking would be unattractive. It is considered to be a finer way of finishing a seam in this way, but it is more time consuming, thus ultimately more expensive.

Ribbing

Ribbing is a knitted band used to finish necks, cuffs and hems of jersey garments, such as T-shirts and sweatshirts. Ribbing can also be found on garments such as bomber jackets, where it is used to insulate the wearer from the weather.

Lining

A lining is used when it is uncomfortable for exposed seams to be next to the wearer's skin. Many outerwear garments also need to be lined. This is often to 'hide' the internal construction from view: interfacings, hand stitching, canvas, etc. With lining, it is not necessary to overlock seams.

8

9

1   A distressed vintage
    Levi-Strauss jacket.
    A new collar and back
    yolk have been
    stitched in to replace
    the originals.

Raw edges and deconstruction

In the 1970s, Japanese designers Yohji Yamamoto and Rei Kawakubo of Comme des Garçons were the first designers to show 'deconstructed' garments on the catwalk. Their clothes revealed the seams of the garment on the outside rather than hidden on the inside. The concept was to show exactly how the garments had been put together. Raw, unfinished hems and edges can also be employed. There is no practical reason for doing so; it is purely aesthetic.

Distressing

The premature ageing of fabric is called distressing. This type of garment finish has been used in theatrical costume for a long time, but recently, so-called 'aged' garments have become fashionable. Distressing a new garment can make it look vintage or it can take away the box-fresh crispness of some clothes, such as jeans.

Garments are usually distressed after they have been made. This way, the area of distress can be controlled and look more realistic – for example, on the knees or elbows. One of the techniques used to distress clothing is to machine-wash it with stones. The easiest way to distress clothing is to wear it (and not be too careful) or to wash or boil it a few times. The fabric can be worn by applying sandpaper or a wire brush to the surface. The garment can be left outside or in a window for other 'weathered' effects. Designer Hussein Chalayan buried his graduate collection in his garden covered in iron filings to achieve a distressed effect.

Tailoring

Bespoke tailoring is the male equivalent of haute couture; clothes are made to fit the individual rather than mass-produced to fit a standard size.

Tailoring is a term that generally refers to a method of making clothes that requires a more handcrafted approach. A good suit requires that much of its work be done by hand instead of, or in addition to, solely by machine. The fabric is manipulated and shaped through the use of hand stitching, canvas and subtle padding to create structure and form; the fabric is 'moulded' to fit the form of the human figure.

2   Chiffon top by Richard Sorger where the arm hole is left raw to fray.

3/4   Basso & Brooke jacket from the Autumn/Winter 2005 collection, with a dart that curves from the side seams towards the bust.

5   Semi-constructed tailored jacket, showing shoulder pads and the hand-stitching and tacking stitches that a tailor uses to mark out important lines on the garment while it is being made. The pockets are tacked closed to prevent them from sagging.

Darts

One of the basic concepts of pattern cutting is how to render something essentially flat (paper, fabric) into something three-dimensional.

Darts create fit. They are triangular, tapered or diamond shapes that once folded out of a paper pattern or fabric, convert a two-dimensional shape into a three-dimensional form. Imagine a circle; by cutting out a triangle and folding, the two-dimensional circle becomes a three-dimensional cone. By suppressing fabric in, the dart helps to shape or mould fabric to the form of the body. Darts commonly point towards the bust and from the waist towards either hips or bottom.

The placement of darts (and seams) on the body is very important; not only do they create fit, but they can add to the style and design of the garments.

1 Black pleated dress with hood by Issey Miyake.

2 The Meret Lurex shirt by Boudicca. Autumn/Winter 2005.

3 The 'Simulation' skirt by Boudicca uses a series of seams that flare to create a 'tail'.

4 Junya Watanabe Autumn/Winter 2000.

Creating volume

In clothing terms, volume refers to excess fabric. Creating volume in a garment means that, strictly speaking, it no longer follows the human form and alters the silhouette to some degree.

Using seams and darts to create volume

We create fit with seams and darts, but they can also be used to create volume. The easiest way to imagine how seams or darts for volume are used is to visualise an image of the world as it appears in an atlas, in which it is illustrated flat like the skin of a carefully peeled orange. Where the curved lines of each section join, they form a three-dimensional globe. The triangular spaces between each section behave a little like darts. If we were to cut through the darts and separate each section, seams (rather than darts) would be required to rejoin them (this is how seams can replace darts). Employing the use of seams or darts to create volume in this way offers endless possibilities for creating form.

Pleats and gathers

There are various ways that fabric can be pleated, gathered or folded. Box pleats, found in the back of shirts, are two folds facing each other; scissor pleats all face the same way. Sunray pleats and the style of pleating exemplified by designer Issey Miyake are more like permanent creases.

Gathering is a technique for bunching up the fabric either systematically or irregularly. Where pleating is linear in nature, gathering can be more irregular.

Volume is created using these methods when gathers or pleats go into a seam or are stitched down, therefore suppressing the fabric at that point and releasing it at the point where it is not held down. Another technique similar to this is smocking; fabric is folded and then stitched at regular points to create a honeycomb effect.

Flare

To flare means to 'widen gradually'. The cut of a skirt can be flared to the extent that it becomes a full circle when laid flat. Flaring the panel of a garment gives it additional volume at either the top or bottom.

Support and structure

When volume has been created, it can be left to drape or it may require support and structure to achieve its full shape. If, for example, a skirt has been flared into a circle, without any support it will hang, only exhibiting its fullness during movement. Supporting the skirt from underneath will force the skirt outwards and show more of its volume. Various techniques and materials can be used, generally hidden within the garment, to add body or support.

1

2

Netting

Netting is a light, stiff fabric used under a garment to bulk out or lift the outer garment. It offers the best support when gathered or 'ruffled'. Traditionally used to make ballet tutus and underskirts, netting supports the classic bell shape of a skirt. Without it, a skirt collapses and the volume deflates. It can also be used in sleeveheads to support gathering/pleating, or if the sleeve has an extremely voluminous shape, such as a 'leg of mutton' sleeve.

Padding

Padding can be used to emphasise part of the body and adds support to create volume. Dior's post-war (1947) 'New Look' collection used specially created pads for the hips to emphasise a strong feminine silhouette (see page 111). This look was scandalous to begin with – the use of excessive amounts of fabric was frowned upon in post-war Europe – but the look became hugely influential in the 1950s. More recently, Comme des Garçons challenged conventional silhouettes by padding the body asymmetrically and then stretching and draping fabric over the top.

Raglan sleeve

A sleeve where the armhole seam has been replaced by seams from under the arm to the neckline, is called a raglan.

1   Leather motorcycle jacket showing the quilting technique.

2   Netting can give a garment support. This is an underskirt.

3   'Atomic Bomb' Tuxedo by Viktor & Rolf from the Autumn/Winter 1998–1999 collection. The outfit is constructed to fit over a 'pillow' of padding. The garments drape loosely without the padding, but still work as an outfit. (Collection Groninger Museum; Photographer: Peter Tahl)

4   An example of a regular shoulder pad (top), and a raglan shoulder pad (bottom).

Shoulder pads

A shoulder pad gives more definition and form to a garment and creates a smoother appearance over the shoulder and collarbone. Shoulder pads can be bought ready-made, often from foam, but the better ones are made from layers of wadding sandwiched between felt or non-fusible interfacing. If a shoulder line differs from the norm, it is best to create a specific shoulder pad from the actual pattern of the garment so that the fit and form are perfect.

Although rarely used in tailoring, shoulder pads for raglan sleeves are also available. A shoulder pad for a set-in sleeve will not work for a raglan sleeve as they are very different in nature.

In the late 1980s and 1990s shoulder pads became quite extreme (hence the term 'power dressing'), before shrinking back to a respectable size, which enabled fabric to simply smooth over the shape of the shoulder and to hang well.

Quilting

Quilting is the technique whereby a thick, fibrous material called wadding is placed between two pieces of fabric and stitched through. Traditionally, the pattern of the stitching is diagonal, forming diamonds, but the stitching can also add a decorative effect. Fabric that is quilted is thicker and can be used to insulate a garment. This is usually added to a garment as a lining. Quilting is also used as a means of protection; for example, on a motorcycle jacket.

Another use of quilting is to create structure. An example might be Jean-Paul Gaultier's iconic bra top as worn by Madonna on her Blonde Ambition tour of 1990. The top references the conical bras of the 1950s, whereby the bra gives a totally false, idealised shape to the breasts.

3

4

Boning

Boning is so-called because it was traditionally made from whalebone. It also reflects the idea of internal structure and support, like a skeleton. Today there are two types of boning: one made of metal and the other, more common, is made of fine polyester rods and is called Rigilene®.

Boning is used to give support to a garment, generally from the waist up to and over the bust. It can also be used to constrict the waist in the form of a corset. Strapless evening gowns, which give the wearer so much shape, and, apparently miraculously, stay up, are supported internally by a corset. Vivienne Westwood's signature corset, based on a 19th-century style, gives the wearer instant cleavage.

As well as the corset, boning was historically used to create 'cages' suspended from the waist: a 'farthingale', worn in various incarnations between the 15th and 16th centuries, was flat on the front and back, but hugely exaggerated the hips; a 'crinoline', worn later in the mid-1800s, was floor-length and bell-shaped; and a 'cul de Paris' or bustle, fashionable during the late 1800s, was much smaller, but emphasised the bottom. More recently, Vivienne Westwood designed the 'Mini-Crini', which successfully married the floor-length crinolines of the mid-1800s and the risqué mini skirt of the 1960s.

Historically, boning was used to provide volume to the garment, but today it is mostly used to suppress the figure, but the technique and the material used endures and is likely to continue to be used in new ways.

3

1 This is the section of the canvas and interfacing that is underneath a tailored jacket.

2 The collar on this shirt has been deconstructed to reveal the use of interfacing in the collar stand.

3/4 A Vivienne Westwood corset.

5 Fine polyester rods woven together called Rigilene®, are used for boning.

Interfacing

There are two types of interfacing: fusible (iron-on) and non-fusible (sewn-in). Interfacing is used to support and add substance to fabrics.

Interfacing is commonly used in cuffs and collars, facings and waistbands. It comes in various weights, from light to heavy and can also be fabric-specific; there are interfacings especially for jerseys (retaining the stretch that an ordinary interfacing would prevent) and for leather (with a lower melting point).

Interfacing should be used anywhere that the natural body of the fabric is not enough to support what it is being used for.

Canvas

Like interfacing, canvas is used to give substance to fabrics. Generally heavier than interfacing and sewn in by hand, canvas is most commonly used in tailoring, to give form to the front of a jacket or coat, but canvas can be used in other types of garment where the fabric requires more body.

2

4

5

Draping on the mannequin

' Learning through action. '

Vivienne Westwood, Claire Wilcox,
V&A Publishing

Some clothes are too complicated or innovative
to be designed in two dimensions; these ideas
need to be worked out physically in three
dimensions by manipulating and draping fabric
on a mannequin (also called a stand). Some
designers prefer to work in this manner; draping
on the stand allows the designer to really push
forms. The possibilities of drape are arguably
endless, limited only by the imagination.
Understanding fabric and its properties is
essential to the success of an idea worked
through in this way – and vice versa. Some
fabrics drape better than others and the weight
of a fabric affects the way it will hang.

When draping on the stand, after the initial
interesting voluminous forms are created, you
must think about how the fabric relates to the
body. Does it flatter the form? Will it move well?
How do the proportions work with the body?
Working in this manner can be rewarding, but is
also a discipline. It's easy to create forms on the
stand, but can they be converted into interesting
and contemporary garments?

1

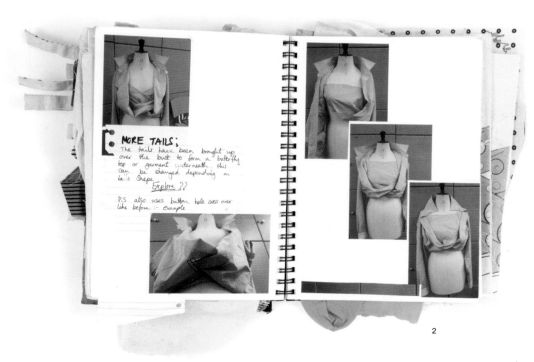

2

/2 Existing garments can be experimented with on a mannequin to create new garment shapes, much in the same way as using a length of cloth.

3 An example of pattern pieces.

Pattern cutting

One of the basic concepts of pattern cutting is how to render something essentially flat (paper, fabric) into something three-dimensional.

A paper pattern of a garment is developed ('cut') and cut into pieces so that when seamed together they create the garment. Good pattern cutting must be precise so that the pieces fit together accurately otherwise the garment will look poorly made and will fit badly. An inaccurate pattern will also create problems for the person sewing the garment together. Each pattern contains 'notches', or points on a pattern that correspond to a point on the adjoining pattern piece. These are cut into the seam allowance of a piece of fabric and help whoever is making the garment to join the seam together accurately.

There are basic rules of pattern cutting that need to be learnt before the designer or pattern cutter can become more adventurous and experimental. Changing one element of a pattern can have a knock-on effect on another piece of the pattern and a pattern cutter must be aware of this. For example, changing the armhole of a garment means that the sleeve must also change accordingly.

Pattern Block

All garment patterns start life as pattern blocks. A pattern block is a basic form – for instance, a bodice shape or a fitted skirt that can be modified into a more elaborate design. A designer/pattern cutter will develop their own blocks that they know and trust. Books on pattern cutting supply instructions on how to 'draft' certain pattern blocks from scratch using a list of measurements that relate to measurements of a standard (human) size. Patterns can also be taken from fabric that has been draped on a stand in order to develop a design.

3

Dart manipulation

The dart can be moved around the body to create different lines, but in the example of a bust dart, it must always point towards the 'bust point' as this is where the fit and form is required.

Darts can also be incorporated into seams; the seam will become shaped and curved to create fit. The placement of darts (and seams) on the body is very important; not only do they create fit, but they add to the style and design of the garment. The following text relates to image **1** below:

a This basic pattern block for a bodice has two darts, one from the waist and one from the shoulder.

b The shoulder dart has been closed and a new dart has opened in the side seam. When these darts are sewn up in fabric they will suppress the same amount of volume and create the same form as the darts in **a**. Only the line has changed.

c By closing the waist dart, the size of the side seam dart has increased. This new larger dart will create the same form as the two smaller darts in **b**.

d Darts can be moved around the bodice to any position as long as they point towards the bust point. In **d** the dart has been closed at the side seam and reopened in the armhole.

e Darts can be transformed into seams by dividing the pattern into sections through the dart. When the two sections are sewn back together in fabric they create a seam. A seam that starts in the armhole and travels down the body in this way is called a 'Princess' line.

f Same as **d**.

Slash and spread

This term refers to cutting a pattern at a strategic point or along a line, opening it up and adding in extra volume. Flare is often created using this method.

The technique of 'slash and spread' can be used to convert a straight skirt pattern into a flared skirt. The following text relates to image **2** below:

a A basic pattern block for a straight skirt.

b A line is cut up from the hem to the dart. When the dart is closed the pattern opens up and becomes A-line.

c The pattern is divided into three sections.

d These are cut along, from hem to waist, and opened up (spread). In this case 20cm is added into each 'slash'. This creates a more flared skirt.

e The final pattern for the new flared skirt.

2

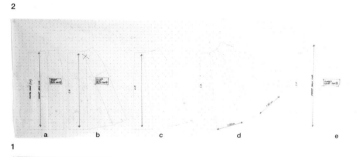

a   b   c   d   e

1

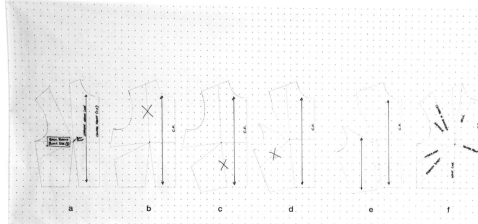

a   b   c   d   e   f

1 A basic pattern block for a bodice with two darts. Darts can be displaced around the pattern block.

2 Using the technique of 'slash and spread' to convert a straight skirt pattern into a flared skirt.

3 An example of a toile or mock-up made in calico and painted with a spot pattern.

3

Toiles

A garment can look very different when converted from a two-dimensional drawing into a three-dimensional garment; proportions, details and fit may need to change and this is an opportunity to make modifications before the final garment or outfit is made.

'Toile' is French for 'cloth'. The term has been appropriated to mean a mock-up of an actual garment. It is made in a cheaper fabric – often calico (an unbleached cotton fabric, in French known as toile de cotton) – to check fit and make.

As the purpose of making a toile, or 'toile-ing' as it is known, is to simulate the final garment, it is necessary to toile in a similar fabric; for example, if the garment being 'toiled' will ultimately be made in a stretch fabric it must first be toiled in jersey. It is essential to use similar weight fabric for the toile as a design cannot always be realised with certain weights of fabric.

Producing good toiles saves time later on when the garment is made in final fabrics, but it isn't necessary to make real pockets or put a lining in a toile. Try to resolve all issues to do with construction so that if you are making the garment you'll make fewer mistakes in the real fabric. A good toile helps a sample machinist to make up your garment exactly as you want it.

Sample sizes

The first version of a garment made in real fabrics is called the 'sample'. It is this garment that goes on the catwalk or is shown to the press. Samples are generally made to a standard size 8 to 10 to fit the models.

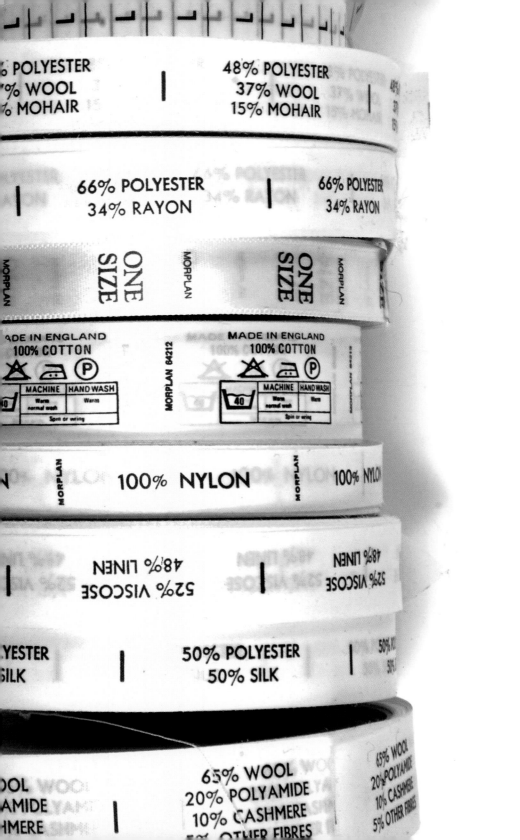

POLYESTER
% WOOL
% MOHAIR

48% POLYESTER
37% WOOL
15% MOHAIR

66% POLYESTER
34% RAYON

66% POLYESTER
34% RAYON

ONE SIZE

MORPLAN

ONE SIZE

MORPLAN

MADE IN ENGLAND
100% COTTON

MADE IN ENGLAND
100% COTTON

MORPLAN 84212

MACHINE	HAND WASH
Warm normal wash	Warm
Spin or wring	

MACHINE	HAND WASH
40	Warm normal wash	Warm
Spin or wring	

100% NYLON

MORPLAN

100% NYLON

48% LINEN
52% VISCOSE

48% LINEN
52% VISCOSE

YESTER
SILK

50% POLYESTER
50% SILK

50%
5%

65% WOOL
20% POLYAMIDE
10% CASHMERE

65% WOOL
20% POLYAMIDE
10% CASHMERE
5% OTHER FIBRES

OOL WOOL
AMIDE
HMERE

DEVELOPING A COLLECTION

Before you even think about putting a collection together you must identify early on what kind of clothes you want to design and sell, and at what level – are you designing for men, women or children, for example? Do you want to design for the high street or for haute couture? What do you want to include in your collection? You must understand the different types of garment and whether they can form a collection on their own or in combination. You must also consider the fashion calendar and how collections fit into this timetable. Finally, you must think strategically about the different ways you can promote and sell the collection.

Who are you designing for?

As a fashion designer you can work at various 'levels' within the fashion industry. The choice you make will depend on your training, ability and interests – and of course how much you would like to be paid for your work. Finding your niche in fashion design may be something you've been working towards from the beginning – or may evolve more organically. But when you start a collection you should have a very clear understanding of who you are designing for.

Haute couture

The couture fashion shows are held twice a year in January and July. The shows present womenswear to potential buyers and function as advertising for the fashion houses. The instantly recognisable names of the top haute couturiers include Chanel, Christian Dior, Christian Lacroix, Givenchy, Jean-Paul Gaultier and Yves Saint Laurent.

Haute couture garments are made to fit to individual customers and are very expensive as a couturier uses the most exclusive fabrics and highly skilled artisans. Without couture these amazing making and embellishment skills would be lost. To learn the specific rigorous skills of haute couture you would be best advised to complete a degree in fashion design and then find a placement working in-house with a couturier. The skills required at this level are impossible to cover sufficiently during a three- or four-year degree course and can take years to perfect.

Today there are very few clients who can afford couture, but it is still an essential part of the fashion industry as the collections are innovative and original, and less restricted by commercial restraints than ready to wear (or prêt-à-porter). Haute couture clothes push at the boundaries of fashion.

It was interesting to explore historical clothes and to think about those textures, those embroideries, those materials and then to interpret them for a woman today, not as costume but as wardrobe.

Nicolas Ghesquière at Balenciaga

1   Christian Dior 'New
    Look' dress from
    1947.
    (© Association Willy
    Maywald/ADAGP,
    Paris and DACS,
    London 2006/
    V&A Images
    Christian Dior)

1

Ready to wear (prêt-à-porter)

Haute couture collections are far too expensive for much of the fashion-buying public, some designers create collections that are high quality, but which are produced in larger numbers to fit many customers within the range of standard sizes – these are 'ready to wear'. Given this, they still retain an air of exclusivity. As the new ready-to-wear collections are not designed for an individual customer, they can afford to reflect the designer's concepts. Ready-to-wear styles are at the top end of the fashion industry. Ready-to-wear fashion is designed by a diverse range of designers, from independent designers through to the luxury super brands.

Luxury super brands

Fashion super brands are global companies. They have immense advertising budgets, their own stores and produce their own perfume and accessories. Super brands also design and sell diffusion lines under their name. They design and produce luxury designer goods and promote their collections on the catwalk during the designer prêt-à-porter shows.

The LVMH (Louis Vuitton, Moët Hennessy) group and the Gucci group are the two main fashion luxury goods conglomerates that own many fashion brands and super brands. Bernard Arnault is the president of the LVMH group, which owns Louis Vuitton, Dior, Celine, Kenzo, Thomas Pink, Emilio Pucci, Givenchy, Loewe, Fendi, Marc Jacobs and Donna Karan. François Pinault owns the Gucci group, which includes Gucci, Yves Saint Laurent, Boucheron, Bottega Veneta, Balenciaga, Alexander McQueen and Stella McCartney.

1

1   Anne Valerie Hash aftershow party featuring a white, gathered dress. (Designer: Anne Valerie Hash/Photographer: Fabrice Laroche /Model: Lou Lesage)

2   Luxury super brand Prada from the Spring/Summer 2006 collection.

2

Mid-level brands and designers

A mid-level brand or designer is not as powerful as a super brand, but is nevertheless an established company that has been trading for a few years with a good turnover and profile. It sells wholesale or may have concessions or franchises, and it may have its own stores. A mid-level brand or designer is usually well known within a specific area of design or within a particular country. A mid-level designer may show on the catwalk and work with a high-street store – for example, British designer Matthew Williamson.

Independent designer labels

An independent designer works with a small team to produce a collection. They have complete control over their business, so they are able to design very personal collections. Depending on the size of the team, they also need to be in control of all the other areas of the business including finance, sampling, manufacturing, press and sales. This can take up a great deal of time, leaving little time to design fashion, so it is crucial for the independent designer to find a balance.

The independent designer may show his or her collection on the catwalk at the fashion fairs. Typically, the collections are sold wholesale to boutiques or department stores, and the designer either sells directly to them or via a sales agent. For example, designer Emma Cook currently sells her collection at London Fashion Week and is stocked in Selfridges of London.

1

1 Examples from the
   Emma Cook
   Spring/Summer
   2006 collection.

2 Casualwear brand
   Diesel Autumn/Winter
   2004 campaign.

MY WALL IS SCREAMING AT
DIESEL.COM

2

Casualwear and sportswear brands

There are also super brands that are involved
in the areas of casualwear and sportswear.
Nike and Levi Strauss are two such brands.
They produce diffusion lines, accessories and
toiletries, as well as their large collections and
many choose to advertise – but do not show at
the prêt-à-porter shows. Casual- and sportswear is also designed at mid-level and as new
labels. Evisu is a successful mid-level brand in
the jeans and casualwear market.

High street

High-street fashion companies design collections
that go straight to retail. They have chains of
stores or franchises across the country or even
the globe. The UK has a very strong high-street
fashion market. The high-street stores look at
the catwalk collections and pick up on trends,
and because of their manufacturing set-up, are
able to react quickly to these fashion trends.
They design and make garments quicker than
ready-to-wear designers are able to – in many
ways because the quality of the development,
fabrics and production is less intensive – and the
production process from initial sketch to final
garment can take weeks rather than months.
High-street stores are not part of the biannual
fashion weeks and they do not usually show
their collections on the catwalk. One recent
exception to this rule is TopShop, which enjoys
some crossover appeal.

Supermarkets

Supermarkets have recently started selling
ranges of clothing alongside groceries and other
products. Garments are produced quickly and
in bulk to satisfy the demands of the consumer,
which means the clothes cost less to manufacture
and can be sold at a very reasonable price.

Founder of fashion retailer Next, George Davis
joined ASDA supermarket in 1990 to start the
fashion-led brand George at ASDA. It is stocked
in over 250 stores in the UK and is now also
sold in Canada, Mexico, Germany, Korea, Japan
and the USA. Supermarket retailer Tesco has
followed suit by introducing clothing lines
Florence + Fred and Cherokee to its stores.

Genre

Womenswear

The womenswear market is saturated with designers and therefore highly competitive. This is probably because womenswear is considered to be not only more creative, but crucially more glamorous than other areas of fashion.

Menswear

Menswear is more conservative than womenswear and is therefore subject to fewer and more subtle changes season to season – for example, trouser-width may alter or a collar may change shape. Menswear sales are also less significant. Men tend not to buy as many clothes and when they do, they are more expensive and longer-lasting. In terms of what men and women wear on a day-to-day basis, men normally wear a less diverse range of garments compared to women.

Childrenswear

Childrenswear design can be just as sophisticated as womens- and menswear, but, in addition, designers must consider health and safety restrictions and the appropriateness of the garments. Childrenswear includes clothes for newborn, toddler, kids and teenage boys and girls.

1

1   Marni womenswear.

2   Menswear from Dior.

' *It's great to tell a story in a collection, but you must never forget that, despite all the fantasy, the thing is about clothes. And, all the time while you are editing to make the impact stronger, you have to remember that, at the end of the day, there has to be a collection and it has to be sold. We have to seduce women into buying it. That's our role. What you see on the runway isn't all you get. That represents less than a quarter of what we produce. Merchandising is vital. We have to keep the shops stocked, looking fresh and seductive.* '

John Galliano, from *Galliano* by
Colin McDowell, Weidenfeld & Nicolson

2

Types of garment

Whether you design for menswear, womenswear or childrenswear, there are different ranges within each collection – for example, casualwear, jeanswear, eveningwear, tailoring, swimwear, underwear, lingerie, knitwear, sportswear, showpieces and accessories. If you have your own fashion company you will probably design all the areas within your collection. But if you go to work for a large company such as Hugo Boss or Gap you will specialise in a certain area – for example, outerwear (coats and jackets) or dresses.

Casualwear

Casualwear is defined as everyday clothes that are not typically worn in a formal situation. Casualwear gained momentum in the 1950s with the evolution of youth culture. Teenagers didn't want to look like their parents and so started to dress their own way. Designers and manufacturers – culture at large – responded, and a more relaxed form of dress was developed, which has grown and become a global phenomenon. The two most common fabrics associated with casualwear are jersey and denim. Sportswear and underground urban style are the main influences on this area of fashion.

Jeanswear

Jeans are trousers made of denim. Originally worn as clothes for manual work, they became popular among teenagers in the 1950s. Levi Strauss, Lee, Diesel and Wrangler are well-known jeans brands, although Levi Strauss is probably the oldest and most famous of these. Today, jeans are a truly international item of casualwear, worn by young and old alike. They are designed in numerous styles and colours. With developments in fabrics and washes every season, designers are constantly reinventing the product by producing a new twist on the classic jeans. Many jeans brands have evolved from designing simply jeans to designing other garments in the casual wardrobe too.

1

2

1 House of Jazz
   coat using jeans
   detailing.

2 From top left to
   bottom right: Levi's
   501XXX, Evisu
   cinch-back, Levi
   Strauss, High Street,
   Rogan, Nudie, Blue
   Lab, Y-3.

3 Stella McCartney
   for Adidas
   Spring/Summer
   2006 collection.
   (Photographer:
   Alexander Gnädinger
   for Adidas)

Sportswear

Sportswear design is different to other areas of design in that it is almost entirely led by function. The garments must perform in relation to a specific sport or activity. This has become an interesting area of design as fabric technology constantly evolves, and sportswear is becoming increasingly fashionable for everyone to wear, not simply sports enthusiasts. Sportswear has its own trends, which can affect main fashion trends. This is especially apparent in trainers, where a functional trainer is adopted as a street trend, which in turn is picked up by fashionistas. Converse, owned by Nike, produces trainers that were initially designed for basketball players, but over the years Converse trainers have become iconic and worn off the court as fashion footwear. Converse is currently working on a womenswear range with American designer John Varvatos.

There are many crossovers between sportswear and fashion. Manufacturers are commissioning fashion designers to make functional sportswear more fashionable. Stella McCartney has collaborated with Adidas to produce 'sport performance' design collections, which include garments for running, for the gym, swimming and tennis. Rossignol, which makes skiwear, commissioned Emilio Pucci and Christian Lacroix – who was their designer at the time – to design a range of outfits and boards featuring Pucci prints.

In turn, sportswear influences fashion design – for example, Comme de Garçons produced its own version of the Fred Perry polo shirt for its fashion line, and Yohji Yamamoto is collaborating with Adidas to produce Y-3. The Y-3 collection includes technical sports fabrics and construction techniques. Many of the garments feature the triple-stripe logo that is synonymous with Adidas.

3

Swimwear

With the advent of cheaper airfares most of us are able to holiday in hot countries at all times of the year nowadays, thus increasing the demand for swimwear. In sports, fabrication and designs for swimwear have technologically advanced, which has allowed for greater variety within the basic garments.

Underwear

Underwear design has predominantly been about technology and function, but in recent years has become more self-consciously design-led. Agent Provocateur is an example of one company that designs functional, luxurious, stylish underwear and lingerie. Unusually for an underwear company, it shows its collection during Paris Fashion Week, which underscores its importance as an area of design. Agent Provocateur has its own store and concessions, and also designs a range for British retailer Marks & Spencer.

Eveningwear

Perhaps obviously, eveningwear is more formal than daywear. Even today, men's eveningwear remains quite traditional, but women's evening-wear is limited only by the imagination. One only has to consider the global media attention on the night the Oscars are held, when the actresses and models make their way down the red carpet, to know how important eveningwear is for fashion and to see how diverse the styles, colours and fabrics are. Eveningwear garments tend to be made from finer, more expensive fabrics, such as taffeta and silk. Eveningwear tends to transcend seasons, and it is less easy to identify an evening gown from one year to the next.

1

2

1   Stella McCartney for Adidas Spring /Summer 2006 collection. (Photography: Alexander Gnädinger for Adidas)

2   Agent Provocateur Spring/Summer 2006 collection.

3   Alexander McQueen Spring/Summer 2001 collection.

3

Viktor & Rolf
Autumn/Winter
2005 collection.

2   Knitwear by Vivienne
Westwood.

Showpieces

Within many catwalk collections, some clothes are considered to be more wearable than others, but you can always guarantee that some clothes will elicit cries from the public of 'Who would wear that?'. However, what many don't know is that these outrageous creations are called 'showpieces'. These pieces never make it to the rail of a shop or boutique, but are conceived to attract the design press, either as part of the coverage of the show in which they appeared or when worn by a celebrity to a premiere, which promotes the designer to a wider audience. As they look, showpieces are intended to grab attention. They are often time consuming and expensive to make, and represent the designer's undiluted vision.

Tailoring

As one might imagine, tailored clothes have more structure and fit than casual garments, and specific skills are required in order to understand their construction. Tailored garments are perceived as being formal, and in many places of work, are considered to be the appropriate dress code.

Bespoke tailoring is the menswear equivalent to haute couture. Each suit is made to fit a specific customer. Many men are still willing to pay thousands for a well-cut suit that will last them over many years. Richard James, Kilgour, Ozwald Boateng and Timothy Everest are all well-known UK-based tailors.

Knitwear

Knitwear designers are really the only fashion designers that develop the construction of the fabric of the garment as well as its design, as they are responsible for making the decisions about the yarn, stitch and silhouette. Some fashion brands have developed from knitwear companies that have their own identifiable style. Missoni is known for its multicoloured striped knitwear and Pringle for its diamond argyle patterns.

1

2

Accessories

Accessories finish the look of an outfit. They include bags, belts, hats, shoes, scarves, jewellery and eyewear. Many brands produce accessories along with their clothing collections to offer a complete look. The customer can style themselves from head to toe in one brand if they so choose.

Accessories are generally cheaper than garments and enable consumers to buy into a brand via the purchase of a pair of sunglasses, a belt or a signature bag when they may not be able to afford the clothes.

Accessories can change the look of an outfit – they can dress it up or down. A pair of trainers with a women's outfit will look more casual than a pair of high heels.

They can also work as fashion status symbols, made desirable through media endorsement. This is especially true of bags, and each season there is a new coveted bag with its own identifiable name and look from the major fashion houses – for example, the Birkin at Hermès, named after style-icon Jane Birkin and the Novak at Alexander McQueen.

Footwear, hat and bag design are specific areas of design which require a great deal of skill in terms of construction, as well as design and function.

With the evolution of the celebrity hairstylist in the 1960s and 1970s, wearing hats fell somewhat out of favour. These days, there are few occasions for which wearing a hat might be appropriate. However, there are a few successful established milliners in the UK. Philip Treacy and Stephen Jones produce a range of ready-to-wear hats, but also design elaborate pieces for the catwalk shows of Dior and Alexander McQueen.

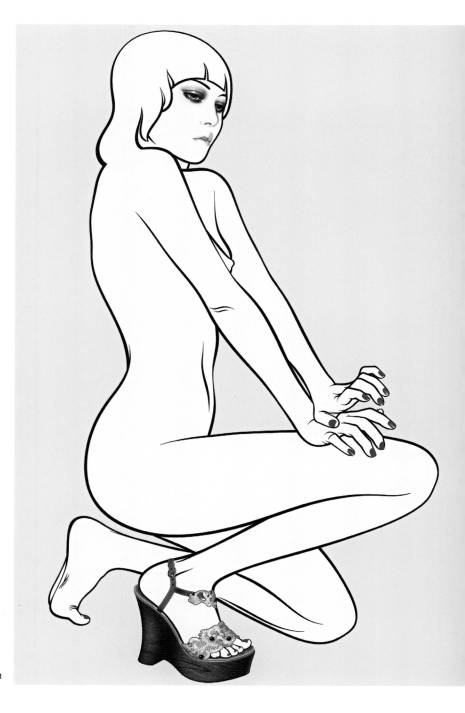

1

1   Autumn Whitehurst
    illustration of a Prada
    wedge shoe.

2   J. Smith Esq.
    couture hat.

3   Chloé Betty bag.

4   Boots by Boudicca.

Chloé

3

2

4

' No one can be pre,
much work is involve
important to maintain or
and sense of self while endur
tough times. It is a pleasure to do,
and without doubt has its rewards
so stick to it! '

Autumn Whitehurst, Fashion Illustrator,
interviewed by the author

Putting together a collection

Fashion design is a fast-moving industry. In order to succeed you must be well-organised and be prepared for a lot of hard work.

1

2

Womenswear Prêt-à-Porter Fashion Year													
Jan	Feb	Mar	April	May	June	July	Aug	Sept	Oct	Nov	Dec	Jan	Feb
Spring/Summer 1 Yarn + Fabric Fairs. Premier Vision. Showing S/S ideas. Start designing Spring/Summer.			Selling finishes.		Sampling Spring/ Summer Collection.		Samples black + finished. Spring/Summer Fashion Weeks. London/ NY/Paris/Milan.			Orders collated + order fabric + trims. Start production.		Deliver Spring/ Summer collection to store.	
Autumn Winter 2							Yarn + Fabric Fairs. P.V + PItti. Start Autumn/Winter designing.			Sampling Autumn/ Winter Collection.		Samples finished.	Autumn/Winter Fashion Weeks. London/NY/ Paris/Milian.
Spring/Summer 3												Yarn + Fabric Fairs. Showing Spring/ Summer ideas. Start designing Spring/Summer.	
Menswear shows are earlier, but delivery times are the same													

1   Mood-boards illustrate 'stories' and are often used by fashion retailers to subdivide collections. These storyboards are by Whistles.

2   Calendar showing the basic Prêt-à-Porter fashion year. In addition designers could also be working on other collections including pre-collections and cruise collections.

Collections and ranges

The fashion year has two seasons, six months apart. Thus, the industry works on a cycle, with a collection for the spring/summer and for the autumn/winter seasons. Small fashion companies produce just these two collections a year, but larger companies produce more. Often they sell two smaller collections that go in-store for the Christmas period and high summer. The Christmas collection or 'cruise' collection can include partywear or clothes for winter holidays. The high-summer collection focuses on swimwear and summer holiday clothes.

In addition to this, pre-collections are produced that are smaller and include a taste of what is to come. These are shown to the buyers just before the main collections. Designers may also

produce a commercial selling collection. The buyers place their orders primarily from these collections, therefore allowing the main collection catwalk shows to be more experimental in order to catch the eye of the press.

High-street fashion retailers introduce ranges of clothes more frequently into their stores to keep the customer constantly interested. This is done by subdividing the main collection into smaller collections, or 'stories', and staggering their release to the stores across the selling period. These are easier to market and merchandise than a single, very large collection. Stories are usually given names – normally a word that sums up the theme of that story, for example: Contour, Zanzibar or Marianne.

A designer may be working on many collections at one time. For example, in January a designer may be showing a pre-collection, finishing the look of the autumn/winter mainline collection for selling, finishing the cruise collection and starting to design the main spring/summer collection.

For a large ready-to-wear company, the autumn/winter collection may have around 200 pieces, the cruise collection 100 pieces and the spring/summer collection 160 pieces. By comparison, for a new independent designer, a collection might be more in the region of 20–100 pieces (15–50 outfits) in different colourways. A shirt designer for TopMan would be expected to design around 50–60 different styles of shirt a season over six stories.

Womenswear Prêt-à-Porter Fashion Year														
Mar	April	May	June	July	Aug	Sept	Oct	Nov	Dec	Jan	Feb	Mar	April
	Selling finishes. Books close.	Collate orders + order fabrics + trims. Start Production		Deliver Autumn/ Winter Collection to store.									
		Sampling S/S Collection.			Samples finished.	Spring/Summer Fashion Weeks.	Selling finishes.	Orders collates. Production stars.		Deliver S/S Collection to store.			

Menswear shows are earlier, but delivery times are the same

' The constant hunger for renewal in fashion is driven not only by a commercial imperative and the consumer's delight in "newness" but also by a fascination with image and narrative. '

Claire Wilcox, Curator of the Twentieth Century and Contemporary Dress collections at the V&A, from *Radical Fashion*, edited by Claire Wilcox, V&A Publications

CB back seem for shaping extend allowence towards top and sew down as indicated.

Side Vent Length 5cm

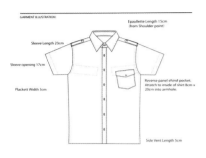

Epaulette Length 15cm (from Shoulder point)

Sleeve Length 23cm

Sleeve opening 17cm

Plackett Width 3cm

Reverse panel ehind pocket. Attatch to inside of shirt 8cm x 20cm into armhole.

Side Vent Length 5cm

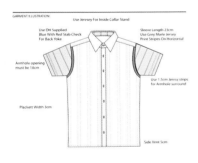

Use Jeresy For Inside Collar Stand

Use DH Supplied Blue With Red Stab Check For Back Yoke

Sleeve Length 23cm Use Grey Marle Jersey Print Stripes On Horizontal

Armhole opening must be 16cm

Use 1.5cm Jeresy strips for Armhole surround

Plackett Width 3cm

Side Vent 5cm

Internal Back Yoke In printed Striped Jersey

Back Yoke In Contrast Fabric

Sleeve Opening 16cm

1.5cm Jersey Strips (As Front)

Side Vent 5cm

2

Garments designed for a season

Garments are applicable to different seasons. For example, coats are obviously more important than swimwear in the autumn/winter season. Fabrics also differ; heavier, warmer fabrics are used more in autumn/winter and cooler, lighter fabrics for spring/summer. However, as many of us work in air-conditioned buildings and live in heated houses the differences between seasons are becoming less apparent, and clothes are becoming less significantly seasonal. We tend to layer clothes up so we may wear summer pieces with sweaters for winter.

The design process in industry

As a designer working for a company, the first task in designing a collection is research. You may be involved with forms of research other than those already discussed in chapter one. Going on shopping trips in your location and around the world keeps you informed of fashion and other cultural trends. Fabric and fibre fairs are important for finding out about the latest developments in fabrication. Depending on the size of the company you work for, you may have to talk with merchandisers and buyers to discuss the shopping habits of your target customer, which garments have sold well and which have not from previous and current collections.

Having digested the research, the collection is designed and a range is drawn up. A specification drawing is made for each garment, and fabric samples and trims are selected. From this, a pattern is cut and sampled. The samples are assessed on their individual merits and how they work in the collection as a whole. The sample may be altered in terms of fit, fabrication and detail and then re-sampled. The entire sampling process may take place in-house or it may be sent out to the factory that manufactures sampled clothes. The designer or other members of the team will be in charge of this process.

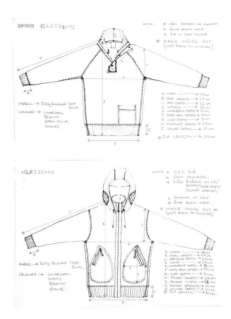

3

From the Chanel Cruise collection. Originally shot for *i-D* magazine, December 2005. (Photographer: Jamie Isaia/ Art & Commerce)

2/3 Working drawings for manufacture and shots of the end result.

Showing a collection

Once a collection is designed and made, your priority is to show it to the press and buyers. It is important to thoroughly research different fashion events to find the one best suited to your product. Try and show at the same place for a few seasons as this encourages the press and buyers to get to know you and to see that you are committed.

Designers generally show in the country in which they work and live – at least initially. This is because they understand their home market and because it is much less expensive than showing abroad. As the business grows they may start showing internationally and which city they choose will depend on the kind of product they are showing and the stores they wish to target.

There are many fashion events around the world. The main womenswear ready-to-wear shows are held during Fashion Weeks in Paris, Milan, London and New York, and the haute couture shows are in Paris. The menswear ready-to-wear fashion shows are during the mens' Fashion Weeks in Milan, Paris and New York. (Which are usually ahead of the womenswear shows.) There are also shows that cover all the other areas of fashion, including casualwear, jeanswear, underwear, accessories and childrenswear.

‘ *It's more like engineering than anything else. It's finding the limits of what you can do when wrapping the body in fabric. Everything evolves. Nothing is strictly defined.* ’

John Galliano, from *Galliano* by
Colin McDowell, Weidenfeld & Nicolson

1

1   Backstage at
     Justin Smith Esq.

2   New designers usually
     show 'off-schedule',
     whereas established
     names show
     'on-schedule'.

The catwalk show

The catwalk show, or runway, is a great way of showing the collection as clothes are best seen on the body, in motion and showing their fit and drape. The designer can create a complete concept with the show through his or her styling of the models and the setting of the show itself. Press, buyers, stylists, possible investors, sponsors and peers are invited to the show. Buyers will make notes on what they might like to buy for their stores. Press will be commenting on the collection for newspapers and magazines, as well as looking at which pieces they might use for photo shoots in future issues.

The catwalk show can be a very expensive event with no direct financial return. The return will only come if it receives good press and if orders are taken at the showroom afterwards. It can cost upwards of £20,000 (or the equivalent). Because of this expense, new designers often try to secure some form of sponsorship for the show. Some high-street retailers offer sponsorship in return for a collection designed by the designer to go in-store. However exciting a fashion show may seem, as a designer it is important not to show on the catwalk too early. If the collection is poor and the show unprofessional it can do more harm to the designer's credibility and bank balance than good.

Organisers of the fashion week shows vet designers and decide who will show on the official schedule. It is usual for new designers who are not on the official list to show 'off schedule'. This means that they can show their collections, but perhaps in smaller, less high-profile venues. They may attract press and buyers hoping to discover an exciting new underground talent. Press will support a new underground designer for a while, but may lose interest if the momentum does not seem to build around the designer and his or her business. Buyers tend to wait a few seasons before buying a new designer's collection. They want to make sure that the business is established enough to manufacture and deliver a good-quality collection on time to their stores.

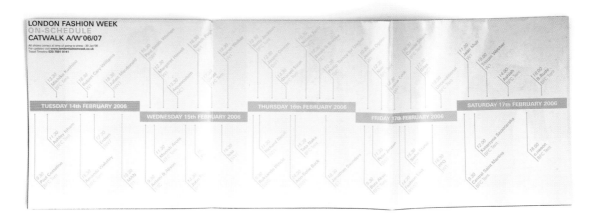

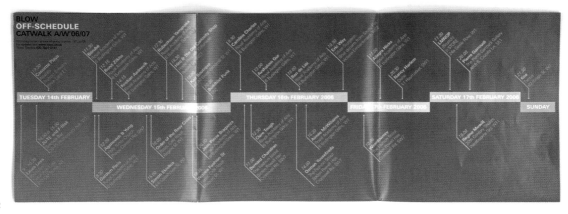

2

1

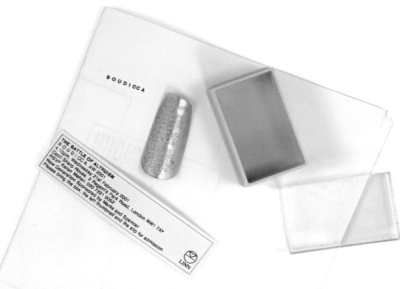

1   Boudicca are very
    experimental with
    their invites to their
    fashion shows; from
    talking invites to an
    engraved false nail.

2   Hussein Chalayan
    Autumn/Winter 2000
    collection was staged
    at Sadler's Wells in
    London.

A catwalk show can take many different formats and there is no single rule or approach. It may be a simple raised catwalk running down the centre of a large auditorium or room with seating areas at either side with an area for the bank of photographers at the end of the catwalk where the models parade up and down in turn. However, some designers choose to show their clothes in a more personal or conceptual way – the show being a very important part of the collection's ethos.

Designers try to find unusual venues, such as car parks, football stadiums, warehouses and subways. The designer must think about what lighting and music best suits the collection and will create an ambience for the show. The guests' invitations and the 'goody bag' they receive when they arrive also help to set the scene and attract the right people.

Alexander McQueen is known for his dramatic fashion shows. For spring/summer 1999 he staged his show in a huge cube containing a snow-covered landscape with his models skating on ice. The show was inspired by the horror film *The Shining*. He has also presented a show where the catwalk was on fire, and another where he manufactured rain falling on the models.

Hussein Chalayan's autumn/winter 2000 show was held at Sadler's Wells in London, UK. He set the stage like the interior of a house, on which the models deconstructed the furniture to create garments; tables turned into skirts, and seat covers became dresses.

Another recent innovation that designers have experimented with is to take their collections off the catwalk altogether and to show them as a film or on the Internet.

2

1   Views of the crowded
    floors at Magic 2006
    in Las Vegas, USA.

Trade show and showrooms

Whether they have a catwalk show or not, all designers have a static display of their collection. This presentation may be at a stand, an exhibition or in a private showroom. Here the clothes can be viewed in detail by the press and by buyers who will hopefully then take orders.

To attend a trade show, normally you must make an application to display your collection and hiring space can be expensive. It is possible to get government funding to show at some of the international trade shows.

The ready-to-wear trade shows are part of the Paris, Milan, London and New York Fashion Weeks. Casualwear and jeanswear designers and companies usually show at the big trade shows, including Magic in Las Vegas, Who's Next? in Paris, Pitti Uomo in Milan or Bread and Butter, which has shown in Berlin, Tokyo, New York and Sydney.

Showing your collection in a showroom can be more intimate than showing at a trade fair. The show room can be in your own premises, in a hotel room or at your selling agent's premises. You may show alone or as part of a group. It is important that your showroom is easy to get to as the buyers and press will have many show-rooms and catwalk presentations to visit in any one Fashion Week.

1

Selling agents

Some designers sell their collection through a selling agent. An agent can be useful as they have contacts with buyers and can arrange appointments for you. The agent charges a commission on orders placed in the showroom. If you use an agent, make sure that you ask for feedback about how the collection is selling. This advice is invaluable and can impact on your next collection.

Look books and line sheets

A 'look book' documents the collection and is a valuable selling and promotional tool. It enables press and buyers to leave the show room or trade fair with a detailed record of the collection they have just viewed, which they can use as a reference later. The look book can take various forms – it may simply be photographs from the runway or something more creative.

A line sheet is a more detailed document showing all the designs as working drawings or photographs with fabric, colour options and prices, which is very useful for buyers.

1 Look books from Jessica Ogden, SorgerKirchhoff and Georgina Goodman.

2 Boudicca line sheets and look book for The Romantic Museum, Spring/Summer 2006.

3 As well as carrying important information, swing tags can be used to extend the brand identity.

4 Bags are another form of promotion for a brand.

Promoting a collection

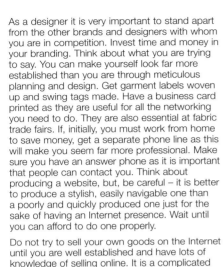

As a designer it is very important to stand apart from the other brands and designers with whom you are in competition. Invest time and money in your branding. Think about what you are trying to say. You can make yourself look far more established than you are through meticulous planning and design. Get garment labels woven up and swing tags made. Have a business card printed as they are useful for all the networking you need to do. They are also essential at fabric trade fairs. If, initially, you must work from home to save money, get a separate phone line as this will make you seem far more professional. Make sure you have an answer phone as it is important that people can contact you. Think about producing a website, but, be careful – it is better to produce a stylish, easily navigable one than a poorly and quickly produced one just for the sake of having an Internet presence. Wait until you can afford to do one properly.

Do not try to sell your own goods on the Internet until you are well established and have lots of knowledge of selling online. It is a complicated business and it's important to remember that you are a fashion designer rather than an IT specialist. A sustainable fashion brand will take many years to build.

3

4

Branding

The brand is made up of a mixture of elements, including a name, product, designer, quality, packaging, labelling and the inevitable 'X' factor of how it is perceived by the public. Some elements of the mix are more important to certain brands. If you think about Levi you think of quality denim jeans and the big, worn, leather-like label on the back of the jean. With Jean-Paul Gaultier you probably think of the designer's personality and contemporary, humorous, experimental fashion. The name 'Prada' reflects an expensive high-quality design and product. The best brands are those that have a strong identity that endures.

Branding is the communication of the brand elements to the target customer, including the ticketing, labelling and the venue where it is sold. The branding of a garment is an integral part of the design of a garment; it is the part of a collection that remains consistent season to season.

All fashion brands have a label for identification, usually positioned in the back neck so they can be seen on the hanger in-store. There are myriad variations, and it is interesting to note how radically labels differ in the choice of font, colour or fabrication – even how they are stitched into the garment. All these things reflect on the designer. For example, Martin Margiela garments are easily identified when worn by the signature four white stitches on the back neck where the label has been sewn in. Garments also have a swing tag that is attached in the store; it has the designer's name on it and the size and style number of the product.

Fashion garments are not packaged in-store – they simply hang on a rail, so the customer can easily handle and try them on. They are packaged after purchase and usually presented in a bag to protect their journey from the store to home. Of course, the bag is also another important form of promotion for the store and sometimes a desirable object in its own right.

1

1 The branding of a garment – here shown through a selection of labels – is an integral part of the design of a garment.

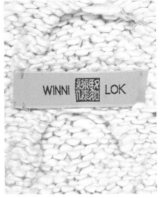

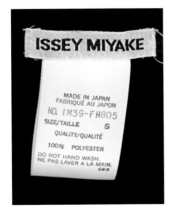

1

Boutiques

Designers with the finance to open their own boutique or store have the opportunity to present their clothes to the customer in their purest form. They can merchandise and display their garments exactly how they want. They can package their goods exclusively and train their staff to sell the collection perfectly. Stores that do this successfully offer the customer a total experience as soon as they walk in the store. It is important that the shop is in the right location to reflect the right image of the brand.

Prada used architect Rem Koolhaas to design their Los Angeles store. It has no signage on the front of the store – in fact, it has no frontage at all, opening out directly on to Rodeo Drive, with only a wall of air to seal the interior and protect the garments from the outside. The store looks more like a gallery than a fashion shop.

In 2004, Comme des Garçons opened the first of their 'guerrilla' stores in Berlin. The guerrilla stores open in an underground area of a city, normally in a derelict building with no signage, and news of the store is spread by word of mouth. The store only trades for a period of time then closes and moves on to another city.

2

1 Margiela's London store feels like little has been done to it to accommodate the clothes. The walls, floors and fitments have been given a white wash and then left to wear and tear.

2 Marni's London store, designed by Sybarite, opened in August 2003. This store has a modern, clean pod-like feel. Highly designed curves and smooth forms lead you in and through the shop.

3/4 Y-3.com and catwalking.com are examples of successful Internet presence.

The Internet

Having a website on the Internet gives a fashion company a strong and easily accessible presence in the fashion market. It provides information about the brand, including a profile of the designer, images of the recent collection, and a list of stockists. The Internet is becoming increasingly popular as a selling point as customers are able to purchase goods easily and efficiently.

3

4

Selling lifestyle

In order to increase profitability, larger brands produce different products as an offshoot of their original fashion line, thereby creating a lifestyle for the consumer to buy in to at various points and levels. Many fashion designers and companies now produce their own handbags, luggage, small leather goods, shoes, timepieces, jewellery, ties and scarves, eyewear, perfumes, cosmetics, skincare products and home accessories. Versace, Paul Smith, Prada and Gucci are examples of designers selling lifestyle. Armani is even opening an Armani hotel in Dubai in 2008.

Some brands have also developed diffusion lines that are marginally cheaper and target a younger customer than the main line collections. McQueen launched his diffusion line McQ in Milan at the autumn/winter 2006 Milan fashion week. Chloé's second line is called See by Chloé, Marc Jacobs's diffusion line is called Marc by Marc Jacobs, Dolce and Gabbana's second line is D&G.

Many designers also develop ranges for high street stores. The product shares similarities to the designer's main line, but is produced using cheaper fabrics and techniques which make the product more affordable. These ranges can be very lucrative for the designer, as well as attracting customers to the high street store. It is a clever move by the designer to capitalise on the success of the name to make more money. Karl Lagerfeld and Stella McCartney have both designed ranges for H&M in the UK.

FOR STOCKIST INFORMATION PLEASE TELEPHONE 0800 652 7661   SOFIA COPPOLA PHOTOGRAPHED BY JUERGEN TELLER

MARC JACOBS
PERFUME

GARDENIAS FLOATING ON WATER, ENHANCED BY CREAMY MUSKS.

1

1   Sofia Coppola lends her face to Marc Jacobs perfume. (Image courtesy of the Advertising Archives. Photographer: Juergen Teller)

2   Balenciaga rebranded to appeal to a younger market.

Relaunching brands

In true fashion-cyclic style, a flagging existing brand can be refreshed and relaunched. A team of experts and designers are brought in to rebrand, redesign and successfully promote the brand to a younger and more fashion-aware clientele. Tom Ford joined the struggling Gucci brand and turned it into a directional fashion company again and a super brand. In 1997, Burberry brought in Rose Marie Bravo as chief executive to make the brand younger and more accessible. She employed designer Christopher Bailey to successfully design the collections and commissioned a new advertising campaign featuring Kate Moss to promote the new clothes. Balenciaga similarly employed Nicolas Ghesquière in the same year to introduce the brand to a younger, affluent market. Balenciaga, which was once one of the top couture houses in Paris, is now once again a very influential fashion house.

2

THE FASHION MACHINE

Fashion designers cannot work in isolation. You may be an excellent designer, but you may not be able to style those clothes to their best potential or you may not be confident selling them to buyers. A designer needs the support of various satellite industries, such as stylists, public relations (PR), journalists, photographers, selling agents, merchandisers, show producers and illustrators, in order to be truly successful.

There is much more involved than just talent when choosing a career in fashion – it's mainly hard work! In this chapter you get the chance to learn from the experiences of people working at all levels and in different areas of the fashion industry. They are all cogs in the fashion machine.

Independent ready-to-wear designer

Marios Schwab

What is your job title?

Designer.

Please describe your job

I create clothes for women.

Who else have you worked for?

Some of the labels I've worked for are Kim Jones, Clements Ribeiro, Jonathan Saunders and Edwin Jeans.

What was your career path to your current job?

I started studying when I was 15 in Austria, went for my BA to ESMOD in Berlin and finally did my MA at Central St Martins [in London]. Since then I have designed for a few labels based in London, Paris and Tokyo and then started my own label.

What do you do on an average day?

I do lots of paperwork, make a few phone calls to do with production and a little bit of design.

What are your normal working hours?

9am to 8pm.

What are the essential qualities needed for your job?

You must be very focused and well organised.

How creative a job do you have?

It has been very creative so far.

What kind of team do you work with?

The team consists of 11 people – some of them are students that are doing a work placement and the rest are people I have worked with since the beginning.

What is the best bit about your job?

The reward after such hard work.

And the worst?

There's no time to play around.

Any advice you would give someone wanting to get a job in your area of fashion?

Be honest with yourself and plan ahead.

'*There's no time to play around.*'

Dress by Marios Schwab. (Photographer: Mariano Vivanco)

Independent ready-to-wear designers

Meadham & Kirchhoff (Edward Meadham & Ben Kirchhoff)

Please describe your job.

We design clothes, make samples, organise production and sometimes get involved with consultancy design work or other creative projects.

Who else have you worked for?

We have just finished designing a range for British high-street retailer TopMan. We have also worked with the label Unconditional and Ed's worked with Courtney Love and Kylie Minogue.

What was your career path to your current job?

School, then struggle and then an urge to change the world.

What do you do on an average day?

Work.

What are your normal working hours?

9am to 12 midnight.

What are the essential qualities required for your job?

Determination and a certain amount of self-belief and self-expression, fearlessness and organisation.

How creative a job do you have?

The creative part is fairly small. Most of what we do is administration, meetings and general organising.

What kind of team do you work with?

There's the two of us, plus a small team of regular students and assistants, one manufacturing plant, a couple of outworkers and a stylist.

What is the best bit about your job?

The small creative amount of work you get to do, the initial research and design process.

And the worst?

All the paper work, the bank, the worry, the worry…

Any advice you would give someone wanting to get a job in your area of fashion?

Get ready for a tough ride.

‘ *Get ready for a tough ride.* ,

Benjamin Kirchhoff
Autumn/Winter
2004/05.
(Photographer:
Claire Robertson)

Independent ready-to-wear designers

Boudicca (Zowie Broach & Brian Kirkby)

What is your job title?

There are no titles at Boudicca per se. There is advantage and disadvantage to this. Boudicca is a life, a passion, a need for exchange and development, demand and failure and exhilaration. A discovery, a search and translation of a new language.

Who are your clients/who else have you worked for?

Those that are like-minded or believe in a difference.

What do you do on an average day?

Hold a business together, find space for thoughts and reading, watching, breathing, examination of everything that makes up the world that we exist within.

What are your normal working hours?

This obviously depends on how close we are to a show. Normal hours would be 9.30am to 7.30pm, but this is rare for a few weeks a season. The rest is what it takes to get the work to the level that we require. To remain professional and on time; you can often be controlled by these demands on yourself.

What are the essential qualities needed for your job?

Inspiration, desire, vision, loyalty, intelligence and motivation.

How creative a job do you have?

Our lives only exist to find creative questions and answer them.

What kind of team do you work with?

From four to 40.

What is the best bit about your job?

That it challenges everything else and ourselves everyday.

What motivates you from season to season?

The adoration and total respect for knowledge and its power. The craving to understand how an idea can find its true perfect place in our world.

Any advice you would give someone wanting to get a job in your area of fashion?

Advice is only what you feel in your heart and that is often dangerous to follow – but never to be ignored.

Our lives only exist to find creative questions and answer them.

Ready-to-wear designer

Jamie O'Hare

What is your job title?

Head designer, See by Chloé.

Please describe your job.

I'm in charge of designing Chloé's younger line, See – a collection, which while keeping the spirit of feminine, relaxed and beautiful clothes, has its own personal identity.

Who else have you worked for?

MaxMara/Sportmax, English Eccentrics, Oasis, Ben de Lisi, Bruce Oldfield, Philip Treacy and Vivienne Westwood.

What was your career path to your current job?

A BA and then an MA in Fashion Design.

What do you do on an average day?

Anything – from sketching to fittings, meetings about the collections or research.

What are your normal working hours?

9:30am to 9 or 10pm.

What are the essential qualities needed for your job?

Creativity, energy and a thick skin.

How creative a job do you have?

It has to be creative to be different to the other brands.

What kind of team do you work with?

Three people work with me in Paris on design and image, and six people are based in Italy overseeing the construction and production of the clothes.

What is the best bit about your job?

Doing what I've always wanted to do.

Creativity, energy and a thick skin.

See by Chloé.

The knitwear designer

Winni Lok

What is your job title?

Knitwear Designer and Head of Knitwear at Whistles.

Please describe your job.

I produce four collections per year: two for my women's label and two for my men's label. These are normally showcased during London Fashion Week.

At the beginning of each season, I will review all the new shade cards that have been sent to me by the yarn companies. At the same time, I will begin research, which comprises of gathering inspiration from various sources. This will be reflected in ideas as to what types of yarn I would like to use, textures, hand-finishing (if any). I will design and begin swatching and experimenting.

I make all the first hand-knit pieces myself and the machine pieces have to be designed in advance and sent to the manufacturers. I will also have meetings with my sales agent at the beginning of each season, to brief him of ideas going forward. I will also have meetings with my PR to take them through the previous collection. There is a lot of liaising between people and organising, as everything tends to happen at the same time… Normally, I will also be organising my production at the same time – always a joy!

At Whistles, my job involves organising the department, which is a huge part of the Whistles' business. We work with factories in the Far East. As the collection is designed in a series of different stories, we have strict deadlines as to when these designs have to arrive in the Far East, otherwise they will be late for selection meetings, etc.

My designs for Whistles have to be very considered in terms of detailing and finishes, so serious thought has to be applied to these areas – this could include beadwork, printing, stitch, trims, etc., and it is important for me to liaise closely with my design director. Whistles is very product-based, which means that even though we have to be trend-led, we do not have to be a complete slave to trends going forward, as other high-street brands are. This means that we have a lot more leeway with the design of the end product.

Winni Lok Autumn/Winter 2006–2007.
(Photographer: Matt Buck/Stylist: Grace
Woodward /Model: Jolyon @ Storm Models)

My job also involves a lot of meetings about
trade, yarn suppliers, fittings. We are constantly
reviewing the collection, as we are (obviously)
heavily influenced by what is happening in retail.

Who are your clients/who else have you worked for?

I have also worked for on a freelance basis:
Hussein Chalayan, Marcus Constable, Montana,
Aquascutum (recently) and currently, I am
working for Whistles as their Head of Knitwear.

What was your career path to your current job?

BTEC at Bourneville Art College, a BA at
Liverpool John Moores University and an MA
at Central St Martins, London, UK.

What do you do on an average day?

Working on my own label, no two days are
ever the same. For example, recently, I have
been busy organising my production for both
men's and women's collections (which includes
getting all the yarns, trims, any finishes that were
used on that collection) to my manufacturers,
which is based in the UK. At the same time I
had to think about and make my collections
for Fashion Week.

As a lot of my work is produced organically and
three-dimensionally on a stand, it means that
the garments are very much about my own
'handwriting', as they develop and evolve whilst
I am knitting the fabric. Therefore, most of my
days will involve making the pieces.

Also recently I've been working for Aquascutum,
so that involved meetings, sourcing yarn, making
of garments, organising, fittings, and remakes –
all fitting around your own label.

I also work four days a week at Whistles. My
average day normally begins by checking emails
that will have arrived from the Far East. These
need to be addressed straight away due to the
time difference, and because the lead-times
with the factories are so tight, we need to
provide any information as soon as possible to
prevent delays in production, sampling, etc. I
then discuss with my assistant the aim for the
day. At the moment we are very busy getting
AW 06 collection together, so our days are

normally very frenetic!

My days are also broken up by meetings,
reviewing the collection and/or fittings, then I try
and squeeze some design work in when I can.

What are your normal working hours?

There are no normal working hours when you
have your own label! The days can be very, very
lengthy, but the upside is there is no one to time
check you when you do have a lie-in!

For Whistles, the hours are 9.30am to 5.30pm.

What are the essential qualities needed for your job?

Vision, tenacity, perseverance, focus, the sheer
love of doing your job and complete dedication.
At Whistles, you need energy, to be a strong
communicator, the ability and an eye to appreciate
small details, being super-organised, the ability
to work in a team, good time management.

What kind of wage can someone command in your job?

Let's just say, when it's good, it can be very, very
good, when it is bad it can be very, very bad! At
Whistles, it's enough to keep me in Miu Miu
shoes for a season!

How creative a job do you have?

Very creative… I consider doing my own label to
be very much a cathartic exercise whereby it is
almost like a visual diary that represents what is
going on in your personal life or in your thoughts.
Therefore, the real talent is to translate these
visions into the real, and something that is
wearable, but exciting. Your ability as a designer
lies in the drawing together of inspirations into
the creation of something original that others
will appreciate, and in the long term, the real
creativity lies in being able to produce things
that sell and/or are desired.

My job at Whistles is obviously creatively led.
However, the difference between working here
and working for myself is that at Whistles, you
are really a stylist. My job is to pull together
many looks and ideas from other designers
and the high street, to create something new.
It is essential to have a great eye for detail.

What kind of team do you work with?

I have an assistant, production manager, a
selling agent and a PR – quite a close team,
but without one, the others would not work.

At Whistles I have an assistant who works solely
with me and then a further assistant who helps
generally with CAD work. I also have a product
development manager, who will track samples,
production, etc., and who also does costings for
me. Finally, I have a technical person, who will
toile patterns, etc.

What is the best part of your job?

The beginning when you are putting 'pen to
paper', so to speak – this can be a tricky time
as well, but it is the most fulfilling time, as you
are making the first marks that set the tone for
the rest of the collection, so this is a time of
experimenting and nurture.

At Whistles, it's working as part of a team.

And the worst?

The long, stressful hours depending on other
people.

At Whistles, working as part of a team!

Any advice you would give someone wanting to get a job in your area of fashion?

Think long and hard as it can take a lot of
determination to carry on. Make sure you have
some money to support yourself and remember
that it is not going to happen overnight… It
can take up to five years for your label to
establish itself!

Working in this area of the industry [for Whistles]
is invaluable and will give you serious credentials
on your CV, so is definitely worth pursuing.
However, the creativity aspect may not be as
fulfilling as some would wish. Therefore, to
have – or to have had – your fingers in both
pies is the best option.

The streetwear designer

Michele Manz

Converse by
John Varvatos
Autumn/Winter 2006.

What is your job title?

Womenswear Design Director for Converse by John Varvatos.

Please describe your job.

I've been invited to build a womenswear team for Converse by John Varvatos to launch their new designer streetwear clothing brand. For this season I have worked mainly on creating the branding and image, which will set the standard for future collections. I have set up the technical system for working as well as establishing an archive, none of which were in place.

Who are your clients/who else have you worked for?

Previously I was head designer of Alberta Ferretti for over five years in Italy and the Creative Director of Womenswear for John Varvatos in New York.

What was your career path to your current job?

I was at the Royal College of Art when I was offered a job by Alberta Ferretti. My move to John Varvatos happened because I was contacted by a fashion agent. Most recently, John Varvatos asked me to head up the women's line on his behalf for Converse.

What do you do on an average day?

Unfortunately, there is no average day for me. In general, if I am in Hong Kong I will be working with factories on fittings and production issues. In New York I tend to sketch, research, put technical packages together, work with PR and Sales.

What are your normal working hours?

Because we are launching a new line my working hours are ridiculous… In general, 9am to past midnight, seven days a week!

What are the essential qualities needed for your job?

Total belief and conviction in the product you are working on. Good vision. Being decisive and not being afraid to take risks. Good management of time and people. A real interest in fashion, film, sport and music, both past and present… All of which are very relevant within our product.

What kind of wage can someone command in your job?

America rewards designers more then Europe and offers better bonus packages. You can expect to earn a handsome six-figure sum.

How creative a job do you have?

Very creative… because I make it that way.

What kind of team do you work with?

I have a fantastic senior designer, a design associate, a technical designer, a production assistant and an intern.

What is the best bit about your job?

Being able to design clothes I have never been able to find anywhere else and travelling to various places, such as Seattle, LA, London, Paris, Amsterdam and Tokyo in search of new inspiration.

And the worst?

Six months of lost social life!

Any advice you would give someone wanting to get a job in your area of fashion?

Make sure you know what is going on in fashion past and present… I like people that are informed. I want to see designers that are creative, but relevant to a modern woman's wardrobe.

The buyer

Yeda Yun

What is your job title?

Miu Miu RTW Merchandising Manager, Uomo&Donna.

Please describe your job.

I'm responsible for RTW (ready-to-wear) buying for our flagship stores and concessions world-wide except the USA.

Who are your clients/who else have you worked for?

I have worked for the fashion emporium Browns on South Molton Street in London as a senior buyer for seven years. During this time I was in charge of more creative and avant-garde collections, such as Comme des Garçons, Martin Margiela, etc.

What was your career path to your current job?

I studied in Paris and came to London to study photography, then by accident fell in to a buying job at Browns – very lucky!

What do you do on an average day?

Out of buying season my days start by dealing with emails, checking the sales of the stores and analysis. As I cannot be in every store all the time it is very important to check the sales reports on a daily basis. Then I will organise stock transfer or reorder accordingly per each area (Europe, Asia Pacific, Japan). At the beginning of the season, I will prepare a presentation for each store. We also organise staff uniforms, sales preparation, etc.

What are your normal working hours?

Usually from 9am until 7pm, but during the buying season 9am until anytime at night that you finish, and often we work at the weekends.

What are the essential qualities needed for your job?

The most important thing is having a very good eye. When you see the collection for the first time, if you don't have a 'gut feeling' leave your job and do something else. You also need very good business sense – you are spending someone else's money and they want a good profit in return. You should be able to balance your creativity and commercial sense.

How creative a job do you have?

Working with a mono brand is less creative than working in a multi-brand store. With a mono brand, you follow the company's creative direction (for us, of course, it is from Miuccia Prada), and the design or visual department is more creative than the buying department. You can express more of your own style with a multi-brand store because you are buying the collection with your own vision.

What kind of team do you work with?

The merchandising team work between the design office and the buying office and they organise our customer services, the production team, the retail operation team and the commercial team.

What is the best part about your job?

You are always stimulated by lots of beautiful things.

And the worst?

You can't do anything during buying season because it completely takes over your life.

Any advice you would give someone wanting to get a job in your area of fashion?

If you are offered a position, even as an intern – take it. Work hard because people will always remember you and there aren't enough good people around!

Vice President of a large fashion company

Caroline Weller

What is your job title?

Vice President of Women's Design, Express, USA.

Please describe your job.

I head up the women's design team. Three design directors and a team of ten other designers report in to me. My job is to come up with exciting, new fashion stories for five different 'lifestyle' zones of the store every month. I make sure that all the different elements of designing a collection (colour, fabric, print, fit, silhouette) come together in a cohesive, understandable and exciting fashion story for our customers that has a distinctive Express handwriting.

Who are your clients/who else have you worked for?

Karen Millen in the UK, J.Crew, Club Monaco, Calvin Klein in New York.

What was your career path to your current job?

Hard work, ambition and a sense of humour.

What do you do on an average day?

Every day is different, depending on where we are with a collection. It might be working on colours, pulling together a concept or going through sketches with my team. There's a lot of presentation involved, selling our ideas and concepts to merchants and the company president, which takes a lot of preparation.

What are your normal working hours?

10 to12 hours a day.

What are the essential qualities needed for your job?

Vision, flexibility, resilience.

What kind of wage can someone command in your job?

Depends on the size of the company, but somewhere between $200 and 400K.

How creative a job do you have?

Very, but within the guardrails of what's applicable for the customer.

What kind of team do you work with?

In the New York design studio there are about 13 designers, a fabric and yarn department, CAD and graphic department, product development and fit technicians, totalling about 50 people. A separate department of merchandisers and production is based in Ohio.

Any advice you would give someone wanting to get a job in your area of fashion?

Be prepared to work really hard, develop a thick skin and a sense of humour. Also, it's a really small world so be aware that your reputation, good or bad, spreads really fast.

What is the best bit about your job?

The camaraderie with my team. Being able to make a living doing something I always wanted to do.

'*Work really hard, develop a thick skin and a sense of humour.*'

Express
Autumn/Winter 2006.
(Photographer: Max Vadukul)

The selling agent

Nancy Stannard

What is your job title?

Partner and Company Director of David Weston Represents, a fashion sales and marketing agency.

Please describe your job.

Selling and marketing designer and fashion clothing to department stores and boutiques worldwide.

Who are your clients and who else have you worked for?

Y-3, Moncler, Jean-Paul Gaultier, Ally Capellino, Winni Lok, Fiorucci, Red or Dead and many more over 20 years.

What was your career path to your current job?

I have always loved fashion and London nightlife and trained as a hairdresser and make-up artist. I worked in department stores selling cosmetics. Because I was such a clubber, I wanted an 'easy' job close to where I lived in the West End. In 1985 I joined a fashionable hairdressing chain to sell their products at wholesale. I became bored with cosmetics and saw a job for a Fashion Showroom Sales Manager advertised in Drapers Record, which I got. It was just clothing, not fashion, but it got me into the wholesale business. When I saw that Fiorucci were advertising for sales agents I went for that. I worked for Fiorucci, UK, for four years. From there I went to work for Wayne Hemingway, then Ally Capellino. After my daughter was born in 1996, it was increasingly difficult to work for someone else, with a lot of travelling, so I set up as an agent working from home. Around 2001 or 2002, David Weston and I merged our businesses together and now have a growing, reputable agency.

What do you do on an average day?

There is no average day. I am typing this from Milan. Last week I was in Paris. David is in New York. We present collections to buyers, write orders, work on sales distribution strategies, liaise with press offices. We can be a designer's right-hand man or simply the one who sells for them. We work at trade fairs, do store visits and staff training, chase debt, pack boxes... It's endless.

What are your normal working hours?

For eight to nine months of the year we could easily work ten-hour days, six days a week. Trade fairs are four days over a weekend of 9.30am to 7pm, then client dinners. For two to three months it can be 10am to 5pm. I often check emails at midnight.

What are the essential qualities needed for your job?

Having an eye for commercial fashion and to understand how retailing works. Likeability helps in any job.

How creative a job do you have?

It's as creative as you want it to be. My partner and I liaise with the designers from the concept of the collection. You have to be able to put outfits together in a commercial way for the buyer to see how it can also work in their store.

What kind of team do you work with?

We are just two partners, with a team of sales people and an office junior. Sales people can be seasonal as the actual selling periods are usually January to March and July to October.

What is the best part about your job?

Beautiful products, travelling and meeting creative people.

And the worst?

Travelling, which always seems to involve 4am alarm calls and working weekends during selling seasons.

Any advice you would give someone wanting to get a job in your area of fashion?

Forget it if you are a frustrated designer. It is a sales job. Learn about retail first as many of the same rules apply.

Public Relations (PR)

Alistair Scott

What is your job title?

Associate Director.

Please describe your job.

I am responsible for overseeing the day-to-day running of Flax PR, a small lifestyle PR agency. I work with two teams, one for homes/interiors and another for fashion.

Who are your clients/who else have you worked for?

Current clients include John Lewis and Laura Ashley, through to Toast, Jenny Packham, Egg and Ally Capellino. My past clients include Donna Karan, Agent Provocateur, Fake London, Net-a-Porter.com and River Island.

What was your career path to your current job?

Following my degree, I did an MA in Fashion Journalism. Immediately after this, I went to work for Lynne Franks PR, which was about ten years ago. I have since worked for a number of agencies and also in-house at Whistles.

What do you do on an average day?

There isn't really an average day. I know at some point I will talk to clients, have client meetings, meet with the teams for a daily update, look at new editorial coverage, talk to press about story ideas and look at the teams' weekly plans to ensure priorities are being carried out, etc.

What are your normal working hours?

9.00ish to 6.00ish. I don't like working late, but quite often do some work at the weekend.

What are the essential qualities needed for your job?

Strong organisational and communication skills. Being able to recognise a story and sell it to the press. In an agency, the ability to juggle priorities is vital. Self-motivation. Ability to get on well with people, as you are in constant contact with the press/clients.

How creative a job do you have?

It depends upon you and your clients. At the most basic level, every PR needs to be creative in that they have to think of story ideas and ways to communicate them.

With some clients you get to work with them on their collections, to make sure they are relevant for the press, pulling together creative teams to work on look books, brochures, visual material. Advising on overall brand identity.

What kind of team do you work with?

I have six people reporting to me. I then report directly to the agency's owner.

What is the best part of your job?

Seeing the impact your work can have on a client's business.

And the worst?

Clients that won't listen. They think they know better than you, even though they are employing you for your expertise.

Any advice you would give someone wanting to get a job in your area of fashion?

Work experience is vital and be prepared to look enthusiastic even if some of the tasks are pretty mundane.

The fashion editor

Kay Barron

What is your job title?

Editor-in-chief and founder of *Rag*.

Please describe your job.

I am overseeing everything, from the editorial side to the design and development of the paper. I am also holding the purse strings and trying to work within a budget.

Who are your clients/who else have you worked for?

I was a staff writer at *The Face* magazine, then worked as a freelancer for *Vogue*, the *Times* and various other publications.

What was your career path to your current job?

The usual, I suppose: Central St Martins degree in Fashion Communication. On the basis of my degree project I got the job at *The Face*. When *The Face* closed I became a freelancer – being published in a national magazine each month really fattened up my Book. Then after months of starvation and misery I decided to set up my own project.

What do you do on an average day?

Write too many emails, ignore too many phone calls, edit articles that have been commissioned and advise the writers how things can be improved. Liaise with the design team to check on progress (usually slow on all sides). Try to write my own pieces, but turn off the computer in frustration.

What are your normal working hours?

At the moment (one week until deadline) 10am until 4am! Not healthy and really starting to show on me.

What are the essential qualities needed for your job?

Patience, organisation, people skills, the ability to run on little sleep and little money. Having the ability to persuade other people to do things for you for nothing and in very little time.

What kind of wage can someone command in your job?

Probably lots and lots, but I prefer not to think about it as I am not commanding lots and lots. Or even a little.

How creative a job do you have?

I am surrounded by creatives and the project is very creative. But I can be writing articles for half a day and then writing a business plan for the rest.

What kind of team do you work with?

There's me, two art directors, a designer, a fashion editor, lots of contributors who are writing/subbing/styling/shooting/illustrating, etc. The immediate group is small and I find it works better that way.

What is the best bit about your job?

Getting in some genius bits of writing or styling and photography, which restores my faith that the UK isn't overrun by Sunday Supplement writers/stylists/photographers, who are so inoffensive that they say nothing in 1,000 words. Also, working with friends, although that can be touch and go sometimes.

And the worst?

Finding out a week before deadline that we can't have certain images and we then have two pages to fill with… something. In other words, people letting us down. It happens too regularly and is really frustrating.

Any advice you would give someone wanting to get a job in your area of fashion?

If you want to write, write all the time. It is the only way to improve. Keep approaching magazines with ideas and articles. Wear them down with persistence. Knock on doors and remember that people will always let you down.

Rag magazine, edited by Kay Barron.

The fashion illustrator

Richard Gray

Please describe your job.

I am commissioned to create fashion illustrations according to the client's creative brief. The client can vary, from editorial – magazines and books – or could be a couture, prêt-à-porter or high-street designer. I am expected to create a rough/line illustration initially, to showcase my ideas and in response to what I have been asked to do. If everyone involved is happy with this, I will then complete the finished artwork, all within a set time and deadline.

Who are your clients and/or who have you worked for?

The designers/clients I have worked for include: Alexander McQueen, Givenchy, Agent Provocateur, Vivienne Westwood, Miguel Adrover, Julien MacDonald, Kylie Minogue and William Baker, Boudicca, Oasis, Printemps. Editorially, I have worked for *Vogue Pelle*, for Anna Piaggi's D.P. pages for *Vogue Italia*, *V* magazine, *Madame Figaro*, *Flaunt*, *The Observer* magazine, *Vogue Gioiello*, *Los Angeles Times* magazine, Sleek, *The Independent on Saturday* magazine, *Mixte*, *Io Donna*, *Jalouse* (USA), *Entertainment Weekly*, amongst many others.

What was your career path to your current job for?

I studied my degree in Fashion Design at Middlesex University, UK. During this period, I was entered for an illustration competition in Italy celebrating the great fashion illustrator Antonio Lopez. I didn't win, but I came fourth, and was invited to go to Milan to meet Anna Piaggi of *Vogue Italia*. From this meeting I was asked to create illustrations for her D.P. pages in *Vogue Italia*, and also for *Vanity* magazine. On graduating, these first commissions made it much easier to get other people to see my portfolio, and I pursued my interest in fashion illustration as a career from then on.

What do you do on an average day?

Each day can vary so much from the next, depending on the turnaround of deadlines and the amount of time between them. I could be researching ideas, creating initial concept sketches, or creating final artwork.

What are your normal working hours?

My average working day is probably between 12 and 15 hours, due to the turnaround of work for deadlines. It can, however, be much less than that, and occasionally be much more, and it isn't unknown to work right through the night if necessary to get work completed to deadline. The flipside of this is that you can potentially also get several days off in a row if you are between commissions. Unless you have determinedly structured your life to be this way, the demands of the job means that it is unlikely to ever be 9 to 5, Monday to Friday.

What are the essential qualities needed for your job?

Creativity, the ability to understand a client's creative brief and what they are trying to achieve from your work, and the limitations or expectations of work created towards specific markets. Discipline to make sure that work is done to deadline, even if it means late nights. The ability to sometimes think outside the brief, and to make sure that your personality still comes through in your work – the reason why you have been approached in the first place.

How creative a job do you have?

Very creative indeed. It's the whole reason a client will come to you.

What kind of team do you work with?

I do not have any team at all, there is nothing to delegate. Any ideas have to be drawn by me, and painting is done by myself. The nearest it comes to teamwork is obviously when the client gets in touch and they will be in contact with my agent, and I will then be given the creative brief by the art director of the client.

What is the best bit about your job?

The best part of my job is the unpredictability of the working year. The surprise and delight when designers or magazines you admire ask you to work with them, and the variation in commissions from one to the next. I think it helps that I have not restricted my career to one single style, so I have a lot of variety in what I am asked to do.

And the worst?

It sometimes feels like there are not enough hours in the day, but apart from that there is nothing to complain about.

Any advice you would give to someone wanting to get a job in your area of fashion?

I think illustration is a career that can be very fulfilling, but like all freelance careers there are no guarantees. Not all people will like what you do, as any art and illustration is such a subjective form, so don't be put off if you find your work is not to everyone's tastes, but always listen to constructive criticism and know when to ignore it. Most of all, as important as it is to be creative, it is important to be reliable. The client wants the work done with as little fuss as possible. Everyone is busy, multitasking, with a million problems to solve everyday. If you make their life that little bit easier by completing your work for them to deadline, completely answering their creative brief, they are more likely to come back to you again.

'Plans for a Woman', fashion illustration by Richard Gray for Boudicca.

The stylist

Grace Woodward

What is your job title?

Stylist/Fashion consultant.

Please describe your job.

'The girl with the clothes' is what one male photographic assistant was heard to call me. It about sums up how other people view stylists. It is a relatively new job category, catering to the rise in marketing and the celebrity, but the reason why I started was because I believe what we wear tells a story about us. Like any story this can be fiction or fact and the reason why we put clothes on in the first place is not to cover our modesty, but to easily communicate ideas about ourselves. I do turn up with the clothes, but this is preceded by weeks – sometimes months – of thought, research and meetings. Frequently stylists work on instinct. Being a cultural sponge, most stylists will not just be able to answer, 'Do I look good in this?' or 'What's hot for next season?', but be able to proffer knowledge on architecture, art, film, design, history, travel – and even football and politics. Stylists create the 'style' and so in a multitude of situations they will be guiding the hair and make-up artists, and even the photographer and the models' poses and attitudes.

Who have you worked for?

I work on a freelance basis, represented by my agent ESP. I consult and style many different brands, from New Look, their in-store and advertising images, to the Dove campaign for Real Beauty. Editorially, I work for many publications in and out of the UK, including the *Sunday Times Style* and *Tank*.

What was your career path to your current job?

I studied Art Foundation at Camberwell, specialising in Textiles, and then in pursuit of a more business-based angle went to the London College of Fashion to graduate in BA Fashion Promotion. Soon after, I landed a job at Agent Provocateur where I stayed for four years, leaving to become a stylist and to pursue more writing.

What do you do on an average day?

Research online and read as much as possible, or shoot.

What are your normal working hours?

As long as I can keep my eyes open.

What are the essential qualities needed for your job?

To be able to see the possibilities in everything, to be inquisitive, to be very thick-skinned and to have strong arms.

How creative a job do you have?

If you work solely for commercial magazines, having to keep a fair amount of your advertisers happy can limit your creativity, but on the whole it's very creative – when you are actually working. In London, I think it is widely believed that poverty equals creativity. I'm not so sure about that.

What kind of team do you work with?

Putting a photo shoot together can mean having anything up to 50 people working on it – set designers, prop stylists, hair and make-up teams, models, photographers and teams of assistants for all of these. Most of which are indispensable.

What is the best bit about your job?

Getting the damn stuff out of my head! People saying that they had seen it, still remembered it and like it.

And the worst?

Returning all the stuff.

Any advice you would give someone wanting to get a job in your area of fashion?

Assist someone good and have some money behind you, preferably a lot.

Winni Lok
Autumn/Winter
2006–2007.
(Photographer: Matt
Buck / Stylist:
Grace Woodward /
Model: Jolyon @
Storm Models)

The stylist
and photographer

Ruud Van Der Peijl

Mickey M, 2005.
(Photographer and
stylist: Ruud Van Der
Peijl. Credit:
www.rudeportraitsof
state.com)

What is your job title?

Stylist/photographer. I used to call it 'style and
image-maker', but people do not understand
that – you have to be clear about what you do.

Please describe your job.

As a stylist, I am hired by magazines, designers,
brands, advertising agencies, etc. to visually
present their products, in advertising, shows,
films (commercials), billboards, etc. This can go
as far as creating images for brands or concepts
for campaigns and shows, but I also put
garments together to fit an outfit and find the
right accessories to go with it. As a photographer,
I make portraits in a personal way (art) and
sometimes work for a magazine or newspaper.

**Who are your clients/who else have you
worked for?**

As a stylist: G-star, Diesel, Casio, Evisu, Nike,
Phillips, Stedelijk Museum, Amsterdam, Centraal
Museum, Utrecht, Panasonic, etc.

As a photographer: various Dutch magazines
and newspapers.

**What was your career path to your
current job?**

Secondary school, Art Academy (fashion),
fashion designer, stylist, photographer.

What do you do on an average day?

I have no average days, every day is different as
I work freelance for various clients. For instance,
today, I am sort of free as I worked all weekend
[it is Monday], but I still have to return styling
items to shops and do my bills and emails, etc.

What are your normal working hours?

Also, there are no usual working hours.

**What are the essential qualities needed
for your job?**

Creativity, personality, organisation (I am not
organised), intuition and good people skills, a
team player.

How creative a job do you have?

Very creative.

What kind of team do you work with?

It depends on the job. I always like to work with
an assistant, so a minimum of two people, but,
for instance, in a commercial photo shoot,
I work with art directors, models, hair and
make-up artists, set designers and assistants.

What is the best bit about your job?

Making things work visually, the teamwork,
the magic… the money.

And the worst?

The fake people, sometimes waiting a long time
and long days.

**Any advice you would give someone
wanting to get a job in your area
of fashion?**

Start working, preferably after a suitable
education (although that's not necessary) as
an assistant, and build your own portfolio
(you cannot do without one – it is a visual job!)
by collaborating with starting models,
photographers, etc. Don't be choosy about
jobs or money, do every job you can possibly
get as well as non-paying jobs and you will find
your way in the fashion jungle.

Internships

Whether you intend to set up your own label or work for a company, it is a good idea to try to complete an internship, also called a 'work placement', 'work experience' or a 'stage' in French, with a fashion company.

Completing one or more internships will introduce you to the fashion industry. You will gain a better understanding of how a fashion company works, and it will ultimately help you to be more professional. Internships count as experience and can be included on your CV.

This kind of work placement is usually unpaid, but they may pay travel or lunch. Newer companies are more likely to take you on as they will be keen for an extra pair of (free) helping hands, especially before the fashion shows. You may be lucky enough to be designing, pattern cutting or sewing, but be prepared to make the tea and run errands. You will gain knowledge by just being around the studio.

An internship can last a few weeks or up to a year. The benefits of doing a longer work placement is continuity. You will have a broader insight into the workings of a fashion company and you will probably also be trusted with more responsibility.

Make yourself indispensable. It is not unheard of for a company to eventually hire someone who has been on an (unpaid) internship. You will also make essential contacts. The fashion industry in each fashion capital is quite small, so the old adage of 'It's not what you know, but who you know' is quite true.

Approach companies by sending them a letter, a copy of your CV and possibly some examples of your work. Try to find out beforehand the name of the person within the company that deals with work placements so that anything you send can get to the right person and follow this up with a phone call. You will hopefully be invited to interview where you will have the opportunity to show your work and sell yourself as an enthusiastic and reliable individual.

If at first you don't succeed, don't give up! You will probably have to contact many companies just to get one positive result.

Conclusion

This book has examined the fundamental elements of fashion design and explored what happens to a collection once it has been made.

It has introduced the process of research through to design, the basic properties of fabrics, treatments and decoration, and the basic principles of pattern cutting and construction.

Fashion design is a combination of all of these elements; a good designer needs to understand his or her methodology and be able to communicate their ideas to others. He or she needs to have an understanding of the properties and the potential uses of fabric, and knowledge of how to make clothes with a view to what is or is not possible. Designers cannot work in isolation and need people involved from other areas of the fashion industry to achieve success, as a good designer is not necessarily the best publicist or stylist.

The way to improve as a designer is through practise and repetition, therefore increasing your knowledge and understanding of clothes. It is also important to get feedback about your work from someone working in the fashion industry. This may be from tutors or other designers, but is essential to a designer's growth. Combine this with as many internships as you are able to undertake as this will improve your knowledge and understanding of the fashion industry itself and the work experience becomes something to add to your CV.

It will take some time to discover who you are as a designer, but once you do, embrace that person. Like any creative industry, fashion is about individuality, and you will succeed as an independent designer, or be employed in the fashion industry because of what you, and you alone, can supply.

Never be afraid to experiment and to challenge convention. Fashion is constant change and without innovation it will devour itself, doomed to repeat trends over and over, as can be seen in its less inspired moments.

We would like to thank all the talented people who have contributed to this book. We have tried to give a balanced and varied view of fashion, and we hope that you find much within this book to inspire you as much as we have been inspired.

We hope you enjoy your future career in fashion.

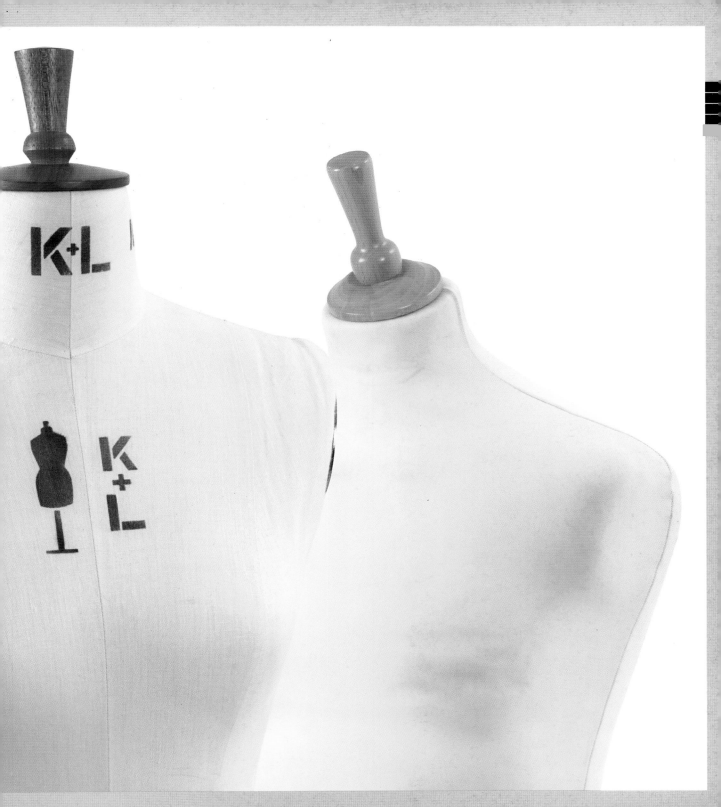

Bibliography

A History of Fashion in the West
Francois Boucher
Thames & Hudson, 1966 (paperback) 1996

Animals: 1,419 Copyright-Free Illustrations of
Mammals, Birds, Fish, Insects,
Dover Press Books

Chanel
Harold Koda and Andrew Bolton
The Metropolitan Museum of Art, New York in
association with New Haven and London
Yale University Press, 2005

Comme des Garçons
France Grand
Thames & Hudson, 1998

Designer Fact File
Caroline Coates
DTI and The British Fashion Council

Erte's Fashion Designs: 218 Illustrations
from Harper's Bazar
1918–1932, Dover Press Books

Everyday Fashion of the Fifties as Pictured in
Sears Catalogs, Dover Press Books

Extreme Beauty: The Body Transformed
Harold Koda
Metropolitan Museum of Art: Yale University
Press, 2001

Fabric Dyeing and Printing
Kate Wells
Conran Octopus, 1997/2000

Fashion Brands: Branding Style
from Armani to Zara
Mark Tungate
Kogan Page Ltd., 2005

Fashion Design
Sue Jenkyn Jones
Laurence King Publishing, 2002

Fashion: The Collection of the Kyoto
Costume Institute: A History from the 18th
to the 20th Century
Akiko Fukai
Taschen, 2002

Fashioning Fabrics: Contemporary Textiles
in Fashion
Sandy Black
Black Dog Publishing, 2006

Galliano
Colin McDowell
Weidenfeld & Nicolson, 1997

Haute Couture
Richard Martin and Harold Koda
The Metropolitan Museum of Art,
New York, 1995

How Fashion Works: Couture, Ready to Wear
and Mass Production
Gavin Wadell
Blackwell Science (UK), 2004

Jean-Paul Gaultier
Farid Chenoune
Thames & Hudson, 1996

Leigh Bowery: Looks
Fergus Greer
Violette Editions, 2002

Leigh Bowery: The Life and Times of an Icon
Sue Tilley
Hodder & Stroughton, 1997

Mastering Fashion Buying
and Merchandising Management
Tim Jackson and David Shaw
Palgrave McMillan

Men: A Pictorial Archive from
Nineteenth-Century Sources,
Dover Press Books

Radical Fashion
Edited by Claire Wilcox
V&A Publishing, 2001

Sample: 100 Fashion Designers
– 010 Curators
Phaidon, 2006

Spectres: When Fashion Turns Back
Judith Clarke
V&A, 2004

The Art of Knitting
Francoise Tellier-Loumagne
Thames & Hudson, 2005

The New Boutique: Fashion and Design
Neil Bingham
Merrell Publishers Ltd., 2005

Victorian Fashions and Costumes
from Harper's Bazar 1867–1898,
Dover Press Books

Vivienne Westwood
Claire Wilcox
V&A, 2004

Vivienne Westwood: An Unfashionable Life
Jane Mulvagh
Thames & Hudson, 1997

Further resources

Fashion Schools

UK

Central Saint Martins College of
Art and Design School of Fashion
and Textiles
107–109 Charing Cross Road
London WC2

www.csm.arts.ac.uk

Middlesex University
School of Arts
Cat Hill
Barnet
Hertfordshire
EN4 8HT

www.mdx.ac.uk

Kingston University
Faculty of Art, Design and Music
Knights Park
Grange Road
Kingston Upon Thames
Surrey
KT1 2QJ

www.kingston.ac.uk

Ravensbourne College of Design
and Communication
Walden Road
Chiselhurst
Kent BR7 5SN

www.rave.ac.uk

University of Westminster
School of Media, Arts and Design
Watford Road
Northwick Park
Harrow
Middlesex HA1 3TP

www.wmin.ac.uk

London College of Fashion
20 John Princes Street
London W1M 0BJ

www.fashion.arts.ac.uk

Royal College of Art
(postgraduate studies only)
School of Fashion and Textiles
Kensington Gore
London SW7 2EU

www.rca.ac.uk

France

ESMOD
16 Boulevard Montmartre
F-75009 Paris

www.esmod.com

Studio Berçot
29 rue des Petites Ecuries
F-75010 Paris

www.studio-bercot.com

Parsons School of Design
14 rue Letellier
75015 Paris

www.parsons-paris.com

Institute Francais de la Mode
(postgraduate studies only)
33 rue Jean Goujon
75008 Paris

www.ifm-paris.com

Italy

Instituto Marangoni
Via Maurizio Gonzaga 6
20123 Milano

www.institutomarangoni.com

Domus Academy
Via Savona 97
20144 Milano

www.domusacademy.it

Accademia di Costume e Moda
Via della Rondinella 2
00186 Roma

www.accademiacostumeemoda.it

Belgium

Royal Academy of Fine Arts Belgium
Fashion Department
Hogeschool Antwerpen
Nationalestraat 28/3
2000 Antwerp

www.antwerp-fashion.be

Germany

ESMOD
Schesische Str 29–30
D-10997
Berlin

www.esmod.de

ESMOD
Fraunhofer Str 23b+h
D-80469
Múnchen

www.esmod.de

The Netherlands

Gerrit Rietveld Academie
Frederik Roeskestraat 96
1076 ED Amsterdam

www.gerritrietveldacademie.nl

Hogeschool voor de Kunsten
Arnhem
Onderlangs 9
6812 CE Arnhem

www.hka.nl or www.artez.nl

Hogeschool voor de Kunsten
Utrecht
Ina. Boudier-Bakkerlaan 50
3582 VA Utrecht

www.hku.nl

Spain

Instituto Europeo di Design
Torrent de L'olla 208
08012 Barcelona

and

Calle Larra 14
28004 Madrid

www.ied.es

ISA Academias de Moda
Calle Andres Mellado 6
28015
Madrid

www.academiasisa.com

USA

The Fashion Institute
of Technology (FIT)
7th Avenue at 27th Street
New York
NY 10001-5992

www.fitnyc.edu

Parsons School of Design
560 7th Avenue
New York
NY

www.parsons.edu

Pratt Institute
Brooklyn Campus
200 Willoughby Avenue
Brooklyn
NY 11205

www.pratt.edu

Academy of Art University
79 Montgomery St
San Francisco
CA 94105

www.academyart.edu

Japan

Bunka Fashion College
3-22-1 Yoyogi
Shibuya-ku
Tokyo
151-8522

www.bunka-fc.ac.jp

Joshibi University of Art and Design
1-49-8 Wada
Suginami
Tokyo
1668538

www.joshibi.ac.jp

Kobe Design University
8-1-1 Gakuennishi-machi
Nishiku
Kobe 651-2196

www.kobe-du.ac.jp

Credits

Photography by Andrew Perris, APM studios, andrew@apmstudios.co.uk: p9, 10, 14–15, 20–27, 39, 42–45, 47–49, 51–56, 60–61, 63, 64, 66, 69, 71, 73–75, 78–83, 84–86, 88, 90, 91, 93–98, 100–108, 114, 118, 123, 125, 126, 129, 131, 132, 136–139, 144, 159, 166–167; Courtesy of Chris Moore at catwalking.com: p17, 29, 35, 37, 40, 41, 45, 46, 77, 99, 113, 116, 117, 120, 121, 122, 133, 141, 143; Courtesy of Richard Gray: Cover, p1, 50, 161; Illustrations from Dover Press: p19–21, 30–33, 62; Illustrations by Robert Brandt: p70, 73; Courtesy of Collection Groninger Museum. Photographer: Peter Tahl. Viktor & Rolf: p35, 39, 101; © Vivienne Westwood: p13; Courtesy of Fergus Greer and Perry Rubenstein Gallery: p34, 36; Courtesy of Comme des Garçons: p38; Photographer: Kent Baker: p58–59; Photographer: Rama. Wildlifeworks: p62; Photographer: Nick Knight. Photograph © Nick Knight. Jean-Paul Gaultier: p65; Courtesy of Collection of the Kyoto Costume Institute; Photographer: Richard Haughton. Liberty of London, Evening Coat, c1925: p65; Photographer: Alexander Gnädinger for Adidas. Stella McCartney: p66, 119, 120; Courtesy of Getty Images/Hulton Archive: p67; Courtesy of Y-3.com: p68, 141; Photographer: Jean-Francois Carly. Jens Laugesen: p72; Courtesy of The D'arcy Collection Communications Library of University of Illinois: p76; Photographer: Nick Knight. Photograph © Nick Knight. Prada: p78; Images from Diesel.com: p84, 115; Images from Premier Vision: p87; Photographs © J. Braithwaite & Co. (Sewing Machines Ltd.): p92–93; © Association Willy Maywald/ADAGP/Paris and DACS, London 2006/V&A Images/Christian Dior: p111; © Fabrice Laroche Images Photographer: Fabrice Laroche. Model: Lou Lesage. Anne Valerie Hash: p112; Illustration courtesy of Autumn Whitehurst: p124; Courtesy of J. Smith Esquire: p125, 130; Courtesy of Chloé: p125 Photographer: Jamie Isaia. Courtesy of Art & Commerce. Chanel: p128; Images from Magic 2006: p134–135; Images from Margiela: p140; Images from www.sybarite-uk.com: p140; Courtesy of the Advertising Archives. Photographer: Juergen Teller. Marc Jacobs perfume: p142; Photographer: Mariano Vivanco. Marios Schwab: p147; Photographer: Claire Robertson. Benjamin Kirchhoff: p149; Image from See by Chloé: p151; Photographer: Matt Buck. Stylist: Grace Woodward. Model: Jolyon @ Storm Models: p152. Converse by John Varvatos: p154; Photographer: Max Vadukul. Express: p156; Photographer: Matt Buck. Stylist: Grace Woodward. Model: Jolyon @ Storm Models: p163; Photographer and stylist: Ruud Van Der Peijl. Credit: www.rudeportraitsofstate.com: p164.

Index

Index (continued)

Acknowledgements

We would like to thank (in no particular order) all the talented people who have contributed to and helped with this book:

Modus PR, Blow PR, Nina Williams for lending from her collection, Art Department, Nancy Stannard at David Weston Represents, Yeda Yun at Mui Mui, Ruud Van Der Peijl, Winni Lok, Autumn Whitehurst, Edward Meadham, Benjamin Kirchhoff, Grace Woodward, Alistair Scott, Kay Barron at RAG, Claire Robertson, Anette Fischer, Vinti Andrews, Justin Smith Esq., Gustavo Papaleo, Neil Bingham, J.Braithwaite & Co. (sewing Machines) Ltd., Whistles, Matt Buck, Linda Ramstedt, Ralph Pink, Shelley Atkins, Rachel Bowey, Sana Uddin, Michele Manz at John Varvatos, Jamie O'Hare at See by Chloé, Susie Boylan at Adidas, Alison Dibble, Hannah Maughan, Chris Moore at catwalking.com, Sybarite, Marios Schwab, Caroline Weller at Express USA, Kerry Olsen at Diesel, Min-Hee Shin, Sophie Hulme, Georgina Goodman, Marten, Moira, Charlotte Wheeler, Amy Foster, Stephanie Molloy, Rie Nii, Jean-Francois Carly, Vicky Cole, Beata de Campos, Jessica Marx, Fabrice Laroche, Nina Appleby, John Trainor, Lindsay Stewart, Andrew Perris, Marten de Leeuw, and Robert Brandt.

We would like to especially thank Carl Downer and Daniel Stubbs at Sifer Design for working so hard on the design of the book, understanding what we were trying to do and doing such a wonderful job of it. Thank you to all at AVA for giving us this opportunity, particularly Natalia Price-Cabrera, Editorial Director, Renee Last, Managing Editor and Brian Morris, Publisher. And a huge thank you to Richard Gray for the beautiful cover image.

Richard Sorger: I would like to thank Gareth Williams for his help, support, encouragement, belief and love. You make everything possible. And thank you to Jenny – it's been a pleasure!

Jenny Udale: Thank you Barry for your endless love and support and to all my friends and family for their encouragement. Many many thanks to Richard, for your drive, focus and Post-it notes!